09-99

Literature & Thought

FROM THERE TO HERE
The Immigrant Experience

Ben Shahn

Perfection Learning

EDITORIAL DIRECTOR   Julie A. Schumacher

SENIOR EDITOR   Terry Ofner

EDITOR   Linda Mazunik

PERMISSIONS   Laura Pieper

REVIEWERS   Larry Bargenquast

Ann L. Tharnish

DESIGN AND PHOTO RESEARCH   William Seabright and Associates,
Wilmette, Illinois

COVER ART   IMMIGRANT FAMILY 1941 (Detail) Ben Shahn
Serigraph, 19.25 x 25.25" © Estate of Ben Shahn/
Licensed by VAGA, New York, NY.

ACKNOWLEDGMENTS
   Lyrics to "America" from WEST SIDE STORY by Stephen Sondheim;
music by Leonard Bernstein. Copyright © 1957 by Amberson Holdings LLC and
Stephen Sondheim. Copyright Renewed. Reprinted by permission of Boosey &
Hawkes, Inc., Sole Agent.
   "Amir" from *Seedfolks* by Paul Fleischman. Text copyright © 1997 by
Paul Fleischman. Reprinted by permission of HarperCollins Publishers.
   "Bananas" from *Jews Without Money* by Michael Gold (Avon Books, 1966).
Reprinted by permission of the Evelyn Singer Literary Agency.
   "Between Two Worlds" by Patricia Smith. From *Scholastic Update*,
March 8, 1996 issue. Copyright © 1996 by Scholastic, Inc. Reprinted by
permission of Scholastic, Inc.
   "Beyond the Pale" from *A Larger Memory: A History of Our Diversity,
With Voices* by Ronald Takaki. Copyright © 1998 by Ronald Takaki.
Reprinted by permission of Little, Brown and Company (Inc.).
   "Going to America," an excerpt from *A Place For Us* by Nicholas Gage.
Copyright © 1989 by Nicholas Gage. Reprinted by permission of Houghton Mifflin
Co. All rights reserved.   CONTINUED ON PAGE 151

SHOULD WE KEEP AMERICA'S IMMIGRATION DOOR OPEN?

The question above is the *essential question* that you will consider as you read this book. The literature, activities, and organization of the book will lead you to think critically about this question and to develop a deeper understanding of the history of immigration in America.

To help you shape your answer to the broad essential question, you will read and respond to five sections, or clusters. Each cluster addresses a specific question and thinking skill.

CLUSTER ONE Who were the immigrants and why did they come?
INVESTIGATING

CLUSTER TWO What first experiences did immigrants have?
ANALYZING

CLUSTER THREE Did immigrant expectations match reality?
COMPARING AND CONTRASTING

CLUSTER FOUR What is the immigrant experience today?
EVALUATING

CLUSTER FIVE Thinking on your own
SYNTHESIZING

Notice that the final cluster asks you to think independently about your answer to the essential question—*Should we keep America's immigration door open?*

FROM THERE TO HERE
The Immigrant Experience

PROSPECTIVE IMMIGRANTS
PLEASE NOTE

Either you will
go through this door
or you will not go through.

If you go through
there is always the risk
of remembering your name.

Things look at you doubly
and you must look back
and let them happen.

If you do not go through
it is possible
to live worthily

to maintain your attitudes
to hold your position
to die bravely

but much will blind you,
much will evade you,
at what cost who knows?

The door itself
makes no promises.
It is only a door.

ADRIENNE RICH

TABLE OF CONTENTS

MELTING POT OR
SALAD BOWL?

In the past the United States was known as a "melting pot"—a land where all people, whether originally from this country or not, were expected to learn the same language and practice the same customs. Like a soup or stew, the human ingredients were expected to merge into indistinguishable parts. Today, many immigrants like to keep their own traditions intact, even while associating with others of different backgrounds. The result is often called cultural pluralism. More than one historian has said that America is no longer a "melting pot" but a "salad bowl," where the ingredients remain separate and distinct. Of course, in a good salad the ingredients must all get along well together.

Throughout history, billions of people have moved to other places, adjusted to new cultures, intermarried with others from different backgrounds, and created a new blend of descendants. Some leave their homelands to find more freedom, more money, a better lifestyle, or simply the adventure of learning to live in a new culture. Others have been forced to move against their wills.

Millions of documented immigrants have come to America by foot, horseback, car, plane, or boat. Many have entered through such historical immigration stations as Ellis Island and Angel Island. Immigrants still arrive in America every day, bringing new foods, customs, products, and ideas. In many cases, they find American companies eager to hire them and neighborhoods eager to welcome them. There are times and places, however, where new immigrants are not so welcome.

Whenever Americans come to believe that the pot or the bowl has become too full, we pass laws that limit the acceptance of new arrivals. The INS, or Immigration and Naturalization Service, enforces these laws. This agency's main battle today is over illegal "aliens," or undocumented residents who enter the country without the government's permission. Some say these newcomers increase the population and take jobs, welfare, and other resources from natural-born citizens. Others feel that immigrants do essential work that those who have been here longer generally don't want to do.

Since people have been moving here from many other countries for hundreds of years, chances are that you, yourself, have a mixed ethnic background. Unless you're Native American, your ancestors were certainly immigrants. But no matter whether America is a melting pot or a salad bowl, it constantly grows and changes in its texture and flavor. The recipe continues to be created.

IMMIGRATION TIMELINE

1820-1840

751,000 immigrants
European population doubles;
Industrial Revolution causes
unemployment to rise;
many leave with hope of
a better life in America

1860-1880

5 million immigrants
Civil War causes temporary drop
in immigration, but some British,
Irish, and Scots continue to arrive.
Chinese are lured by Gold Rush and
by work on railroads during
westward expansion.

*1879—Naturalization Act bars Asians
from becoming citizens*

1900-1920

14.5 million immigrants
Italians, Greeks, Austrians,
Hungarians, and Russians
continue to pour in; Mexican
laborers cross borders to
work on farms and railroads

*1917—Immigration Act exclu
all Asians, raises head
tax, and establishes
original-language liter
tests for all immigrant
over 16 years old*

1840-1860

4 million immigrants
Northern and western Europeans
emigrate; starving people leave
famine in Sweden and potato
famine in Ireland; failed political
revolutions send Germans into
exile; emigration feasible for
many with faster, more
affordable steamships

*1845—Anti-immigrant "Know-
Nothing" Party founded
but dies within ten years*

1880-1900

9 million immigrants
Southern and eastern Europeans
emigrate for financial reasons;
Jews flee persecution in Russia

*1882—Chinese Exclusion Act
bars Chinese and sets
"head tax" on immigrants*

*1891—Bureau of
Immigration
set up*
*1892—Ellis Island
Processing
Center opens*

1980–2000

16.5 million immigrants (estimated)
Asians and Latin Americans emigrate to escape revolutions and economic instability; Nigerians and Bosnians flee civil wars; number of undocumented aliens in America soars

1980—New Refugee Act sets criteria for refugee admission

1986—Immigration Reform Control Act sets penalties for hiring illegal aliens but provides amnesty for some illegals already in U.S.

1990—Reform Act raises limit on total immigration

1998—Immigration Act makes it harder for illegal immigrants to stay in America

1940–1960

3.5 million immigrants
Foreign-born population decreases; Korean and East European war refugees allowed in; Japanese placed in internment camps during WWII

1943—Chinese exclusion laws repealed

1948—Displaced Persons Act admits European refugees

1950—Internal Security Act deports "subversives"; aliens must report addresses annually

1952—Immigration and Nationality Act restricts Eastern Hemisphere immigrants; preference given to skilled workers

1920–1940

4.6 million immigrants
Great Depression causes drop in immigration—more leave America than arrive, but Polish, Romanian, and other eastern Europeans emigrate to escape Communism

1921—Emergency Quota Act limits number of immigrants from different countries

1924—National Origins Act shows bias against Asians and eastern or southern Europeans

1960–1980

**8 million immigrants
(not including illegals)**
Era of many "boat people" begins: Cuban and S.E. Asian refugees flee war and political upheaval; Cambodians escape massacres; resettlement programs start in U.S. and other countries

1965—Immigration and Nationality Act ends old quota system, opens door to Asians

1978—Immigration and Nationality Act deports Nazi persecutors and combines Western and Eastern Hemisphere immigrant limits

CONCEPT VOCABULARY

You will find the following terms and definitions useful as you read and discuss the selections in this book.

assimilation the process of fitting in to a new culture or becoming like others in that culture

asylum protection granted by one nation to a refugee from another nation, usually due to political unrest in the refugee's native land

diversity variety; differences. In the study of human culture, diversity refers to the differences between human societies and individuals.

emigration the act of leaving a country to settle elsewhere

ethnicity common group characteristics based on race, nationality, religion, or language

forced immigration going to another country against one's will; the American slave system is an example

"green card" a work permit given to legal immigrants who have not yet become citizens

greenhorn a newcomer unacquainted with customs and culture

illegal immigrant refers to any immigrant who does not go through the correct legal procedure to live and work in a country; other terms are "illegal alien" or "undocumented foreigner"

immigration the act of entering a country to live there

INS Immigration and Naturalization Service; the American agency that regulates the flow of immigration by enforcing U.S. immigration laws

legal immigrant refers to any immigrant who goes through the correct legal procedure to live and work in a country

migration movement from one place to another

naturalization the process in which an immigrant gains the rights of a natural-born citizen

passport a legal permit to leave the country of citizenship

pluralism a condition in society in which many ethnic, religious, or social groups coexist within a common civilization while keeping individual traditions

quota system governmental regulation which allows a limited number of immigrants per year

refugee a person who flees from a place to escape danger or persecution

visa a legal permit to enter a country

CLUSTER ONE

Who Were the Immigrants and Why Did They Come?

Thinking Skill INVESTIGATING

THE NEW COLOSSUS

EMMA LAZARUS

Not like the brazen giant of Greek fame,
With conquering limbs astride from land to land;[1]
Here at our sea-washed sunset gates shall stand
A mighty woman with a torch, whose flame
Is the imprisoned lightning, and her name
Mother of Exiles. From her beacon-hand
Glows world-wide welcome; her mild eyes command
The air-bridged harbor that twin-cities frame.
"Keep, ancient lands, your storied pomp!"[2] cries she
With silent lips. "Give me your tired, your poor,
Your huddled masses yearning to breathe free,
The wretched refuse of your teeming shore.
Send these, the homeless, tempest-tossed to me—
I lift my lamp beside the golden door!"

1 a reference to the Colossus of Rhodes, an enormous bronze statue that
 stood overlooking the harbor of Rhodes around 200 B.C.
2 **storied pomp:** legendary history of elaborate or pompous people and
 celebrations

General Considerations
for the Plantation
in New England

John Winthrop et al.

In the late 1620s, Puritan leaders in England began planning a plantation, or colony, in the New World. As part of their campaign to attract settlers, they distributed a pamphlet listing reasons why people should emigrate to the New World. In 1630, perhaps influenced by this literature, several thousand people boarded ships bound for America. John Winthrop, who later became the first governor of Massachusetts, is generally considered the main writer of this pamphlet.

First, it will be a service to the Church of great consequence, to carry the Gospel into those parts of the world. . . .

Secondly, all other churches of Europe are brought to desolation, and it may be justly feared that the like judgment is coming upon us; and who knows but that God hath provided this place to be a refuge for many whom he means to save out of the general destruction?

Thirdly, the land grows weary of her inhabitants, so that man, which is the most precious of all creatures, is here more vile and base than the earth they tread upon; so as children, neighbors and friends, especially of the poor, are counted the greatest burdens, which, if things were right, would be the chiefest earthly blessings.

fourthly, we are grown to that excess and intemperance in all excess of riot, as no mean estate almost will suffice. . . . Hence it comes to pass, that all arts and trades are carried . . . as it is almost impossible for a good, upright man to maintain his charge, and live comfortably in any of them.

fifthly, the schools of learning and religion are so corrupted as . . . most children, even the best, wittiest, and of fairest hopes, are perverted, corrupted, and utterly overthrown by the multitude of evil examples. . . .

Sixthly, the whole earth is the Lord's garden, and he hath given it to the sons of Adam to be tilled and improved by them. Why then should we stand starving here for places of habitation . . . and in the mean time suffer whole countries, as profitable for the use of man, to lie waste without any improvement?

Seventhly, what can be better work, and more noble, and worthy a Christian, than to help to raise and support a particular church while it is in its infancy. . . .

Eighthly, if any such as are known to be godly, and live in wealth and prosperity here, shall forsake all this to join themselves with this church, and run in hazard with them of a hard and mean condition, it will be an example of great use both for the removing of scandal and sinister and worldly respects, to give more life to the faith of God's people in their prayers for the Plantation, and also to encourage others to join the more willingly in it.

Ben Shahn

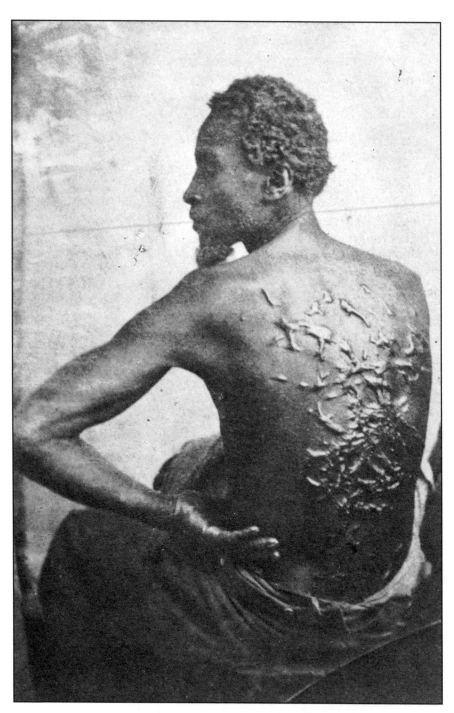

A gruesome network of scars bears witness to severe beatings.

A SLAVE NARRATIVE

GUSTAVUS VASSA

From 1619 until the slave trade was outlawed in 1808, millions of
Africans were brought to America against their will. In an autobiography
written in 1791, Gustavus Vassa (formerly named Olaudah Equiano),
recounts his capture and forced immigration to the United States.
This narrative begins shortly before he is carried aboard a slave ship.

The first object which saluted my eyes when I arrived on the coast, was the sea, and a slave ship, which was then riding at anchor, and waiting for its cargo. These filled me with astonishment, which was soon converted into terror, when I was carried on board. I was immediately handled, and tossed up to see if I were sound, by some of the crew; and I was now persuaded that I had gotten into a world of bad spirits, and that they were going to kill me. Their complexions, too, differing so much from ours, their long hair, and the language they spoke (which was very different from any I had ever heard), united to confirm me in this belief. Indeed, such were the horrors of my views and fears at the moment, that, if ten thousand worlds had been my own, I would have freely parted with them all to have exchanged my condition with that of the meanest slave in my own country. When I looked round the ship too, and saw a large furnace of copper boiling, and a multitude of black people of every description chained together, every one of their countenances expressing dejection and sorrow, I no longer doubted of my fate; and, quite overpowered with horror and anguish, I fell motionless on the deck and fainted. When I recovered a little, I found some black people about me, who I believed were some of those who had brought me on board, and had been receiving their pay; they talked to me in order to cheer me, but all in vain. I asked them if we were not to be eaten by those white men with horrible looks, red faces, and long hair. They told me I was not, and one of the crew brought me a small portion of spirituous liquor in a wine glass; but, being afraid of him, I would not take it out of his hand. One of the blacks, therefore, took it from him and gave it to me, and I took a little down my palate,[1] which, instead of reviving me, as they thought it would, threw me into the greatest consternation at the strange feeling it produced, having never tasted any such liquor before. Soon after this, the blacks who brought me on board went off, and left me abandoned to despair.

I now saw myself deprived of all chance of returning to my native country, or even the least glimpse of hope of gaining the shore, which I now considered as friendly. . . . I was soon put down under the decks, and there I received such a salutation in my nostrils as I had never experienced in my life: so that, with the loathsomeness of the stench, and crying together, I became so sick and low that I was not able to eat, nor had I the least desire to taste anything. I now wished for the last friend, death, to relieve me; but soon, to my grief, two of the white men offered me eatables; and, on my refusing to eat, one of them held me fast by the hands, and laid me across, I think, the windlass,[2] and tied my feet, while the other flogged[3] me severely. I had never experienced anything of this kind before, and, although not being used to the water, I naturally feared that element the first time I saw it, yet, nevertheless, could I have got over the nettings, I would have jumped over the side, but I could not; and besides, the crew used to watch us very closely who were not chained down to the decks, lest we should leap into the water; and I have seen some of these poor African prisoners most severely cut, for attempting to do so, and hourly whipped for not eating. This indeed was often the case with myself. In a little time after, amongst the poor chained men, I found some of my own nation, which in a small degree gave ease to my mind. I inquired of these what was to be done with us? They gave me to understand, we were to be carried to these white people's country to work for them. I then was a little revived, and thought, if it were no worse than

---

1 **palate:** roof of the mouth; also refers to the sense of taste
2 **windlass:** horizontal board or barrel used to pull up a ship's anchor
3 **flogged:** beat severely with a rod or whip

working, my situation was not so desperate; but still I feared I should be put to death, the white people looked and acted, as I thought, in so savage a manner; for I had never seen among any people such instances of brutal cruelty; and this not only shown towards us blacks, but also to some of the whites themselves. One white man in particular I saw, when we were permitted to be on deck, flogged so unmercifully with a large rope near the foremast,[4] that he died in consequence of it; and they tossed him over the side as they would have done a brute. This made me fear these people the more; and I expected nothing less than to be treated in the same

Africans on the slave deck of the 19th century ship *Wildfire*.

manner. I could not help expressing my fears and apprehensions to some of my countrymen; I asked them if these people had no country, but lived in this hollow place (the ship)? They told me they did not, but came from a distant one. "Then," said I, "how comes it in all our country we never heard of them?" They told me because they lived so very far off. . . .

At last, when the ship we were in, had got in all her cargo, they made ready with many fearful noises, and we were all put under deck, so that we could not see how they managed the vessel. But this disappointment was the least of my sorrow. The stench of the hold while we were on the coast was so intolerably loathsome, that it was dangerous to remain there for any time, and some of us had been permitted to stay on the

4 **foremast:** the tallest mast near the forward part of a ship

deck for the fresh air; but now that the whole ship's cargo were confined together, it became absolutely pestilential.[5] The closeness of the place, and the heat of the climate, added to the number in the ship . . . and brought on a sickness among the slaves, of which many died. . . . The shrieks of the women, and the groans of the dying, rendered the whole a scene of horror almost inconceivable. Happily perhaps, for myself, I was soon reduced so low here that it was thought necessary to keep me almost always on deck; and from my extreme youth I was not put in fetters.[6] In this situation I expected every hour to share the fate of my companions, some of whom were almost daily brought upon deck at the point of death, which I began to hope would soon put an end to my miseries. Often did I think many of the inhabitants of the deep much more happy than myself. I envied them the freedom they enjoyed, and as often wished I could change my condition for theirs. Every circumstance I met with, served only to render my state more painful, and heightened my apprehensions, and my opinion of the cruelty of the whites.

. . . At last, we came in sight of [land], at which the whites on board gave a great shout, and made many signs of joy to us. We did not know what to think of this; but as the vessel drew nearer, we plainly saw the harbor, and other ships of different kinds and sizes, and we soon anchored amongst them. . . . Many merchants and planters now came on board, though it was in the evening. They put us in separate parcels, and examined us attentively. They also made us jump, and pointed to the land, signifying we were to go there. We thought by this, we should be eaten by these ugly men, as they appeared to us; and, when soon after we were all put down under the deck again, there was much dread and trembling among us, and nothing but bitter cries to be heard all the night from these apprehensions, insomuch, that at last the white people got some old slaves from the land to pacify us. They told us we were not to be eaten, but to work, and were soon to go on land, where we would see many of our country people. This report eased us much. And sure enough, soon after we were landed, there came to us Africans of all languages.

We were conducted immediately to the merchant's yard, where we were all pent up together, like so many sheep in a fold, without regard to sex or age. . . .

5 **pestilential:** harmful; deadly
6 **fetters:** chains or shackles for the feet

We were not many days in the merchant's custody, before we were sold after their usual manner, which is this: On a signal given (as the beat of a drum), the buyers rush at once into the yard where the slaves are confined, and make choice of that parcel they like best. The noise and clamor with which this attended, and the eagerness visible in the countenances of the buyers, serve not a little to increase the apprehension of terrified Africans. . . . In this manner, without scruple, are relations and friends separated, most of them never to see each other again. I remember, in the vessel in which I was brought over, in the men's apartment, there were several brothers, who, in the sale, were sold in different lots; and it was very moving on this occasion, to see and hear their cries at parting. . . . Is it not enough that we are torn from our country and friends, to toil for your luxury and lust of gain? . . . Are the dearest friends and relations . . . still to be parted from each other, and thus prevented from cheering the gloom of slavery, with the small comfort of being together, and mingling their sufferings and sorrows? Why are parents to lose their children, brothers their sisters, or husbands their wives? Surely, this is a new refinement in cruelty, which . . . thus aggravates distress, and adds fresh horrors even to the wretchedness of slavery. ∾

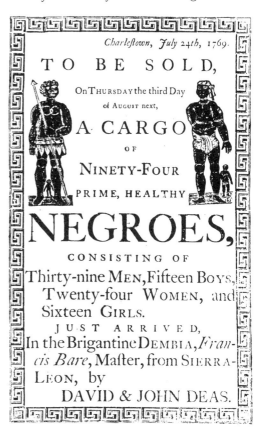

OLD SKIBBEREEN

ANONYMOUS

*Many Irish songs originated in the mid-1800s, lamenting the widespread
potato famine. Potatoes were the mainstay of Irish diets at that time,
much as bread would be to us today. Scores of people died and
many others left the country in search of a better life elsewhere.*

Oh, father dear, I often hear you speak of Erin's Isle,[1]
Her lofty scenes and valleys green, her mountains rude and wild,
They say it is a lovely land wherein a prince might dwell,
Oh, why did you abandon it? The reason to me tell.

Oh, son! I loved my native land with energy and pride,
Till a blight[2] came o'er my crops—my sheep, my cattle died;
My rent and taxes were too high, I could not them redeem,
And that's the cruel reason that I left old Skibbereen.[3]

Oh, well do I remember the bleak December day,
The landlord and the sheriff came to drive us all away;
They set my roof on fire with their cursed English spleen,[4]
And that's another reason that I left old Skibbereen.

1 **Erin's Isle:** another name for the island of Ireland
2 **blight:** plant disease resulting in withered crops
3 **Skibbereen:** town in Ireland
4 **spleen:** anger; ill will

Your mother, too, God rest her soul, fell on the snowy ground,
She fainted in her anguish, seeing the desolation round,
She never rose, but passed away from life to mortal dream,
And found a quiet grave, my boy, in dear old Skibbereen.

And you were only two years old and feeble was your frame,
I could not leave you with my friends, you bore your father's name—
I wrapt you in my cotamore[5] at the dead of night unseen,
I heaved a sigh and bade good-bye, to dear old Skibbereen.

5 **cotamore:** overcoat

GOLD MOUNTAIN POEMS

ANONYMOUS

During the 1850s, thousands of Chinese fled poverty to seek wealth in the gold fields of California, or Gold Mountain, as the Chinese referred to it. In 1882, however, the Chinese Exclusion Act prohibited the entry of common laborers. Prospective Chinese immigrants were locked in wooden barracks on Angel Island to be processed. There they underwent a physical exam and interrogation. The few non-laborers who passed were ferried to San Francisco to begin a new life; laborers were summarily deported back to China. Detainees sometimes waited weeks or months to be processed. While waiting, many wrote poems on the walls of the barracks. In the 1930s, two detainees copied some of these poems, preserving the lamentations of the prisoners at Angel Island.

The moment I hear
     we've entered the port,
I am all ready:
     my belongings wrapped in a bundle.
Who would have expected joy to become sorrow:
Detained in a dark, crude, filthy room?
What can I do?
Cruel treatment, not one restful breath of air.
Scarcity of food, severe restrictions—all
     unbearable.
Here even a proud man bows his head low.

At home I was in poverty,
     constantly worried about firewood and rice.
I borrowed money
     to come to Gold Mountain.
Immigration officers cross-examined me;
     no way could I get through.
Deported to this island,
     like a convicted criminal.
Here—
Mournful sighs fill the gloomy room.
A nation weak; her people often humiliated
Like animals, tortured and destroyed at others'
     whim.

THE POGROMS WERE
ALL AROUND US

SHMUEL GOLDMAN, WITH MILTON MELTZER

Shmuel Goldman was an immigrant tailor from Poland—then part of the huge Russian empire—who ended his days in California. "The deepest impressions of my life," he told an interviewer, "are where the roots are set." In his old age he goes back in memory to his youthful years in the shtetl, the small town he came from.

Anti-Semitism was an ancient tradition in Russia. Under the Czar Jews were humiliated and hounded by hundreds of restrictions. Military conscription of Jews was especially heavy—boys were drafted into the army for twenty-five years of service. Whatever the Russian people suffered—poverty, hunger, misfortune—was always blamed on the Jews.

The Russian way of "solving the Jewish problem" was to treat this people like the plague. From 1804 the Jews were forced to live as though quarantined,[1] in a confined region called the Pale of Settlement. It was a rigid policy of segregation designed to save the "Holy" Russian people from contamination by the Jews.

When Czar Alexander II was murdered in 1881, the false charge that "the Jews did it" was rumored everywhere. Pogroms—the organized massacre of helpless people—broke out in many places and tens of thousands of Jews were injured or killed.

Shmuel Goldman tells us why his family was among the 3 million Jews who between 1880 and 1924 joined the mass flight from persecution and poverty.

---

1 **quarantined:** enforced isolation from others

THE POGRAM
1931
Marc Chagall   PERSONAL NARRATIVE   **29**

Oh, how often in our dreams, like a bird, we fly back to the place of our birth, to that little Polish town on the Vistula, which would be to you a small speck on the map, maybe even too insignificant for a map. A few thousand people huddled together, hidden in the hills, but with a view in sight of the beautiful river. In this place, the population was nearly equal Poles and Jews. All were poor. There were the poor and the poorer still.

If you walked through the Jewish quarter, you would see small houses, higgledy-piggledy, leaning all over each other. Some had straw roofs; if shingles, some broken. No cobbles on the streets, and you might not even want to call them streets, so narrow and deep-rutted from wagons. Everywhere children, cats, geese, chickens, sometimes a goat, altogether making very strong smells and noises. Always the children were dirty and barefoot, always the dogs were skinny and mean, not Jewish dogs. They came over from Gentile quarters looking for garbage and cats. You would go along this way until you crossed the wooden bridge into the main platz.[2] Here were the women on market day, sitting in the open, or in little wooden stalls if they were well-off. Around the platz, a few Jewish stores, a stable, the pump with a roof and a bench.

Most important, you would see here two buildings, facing each other on opposite sides of the platz, without smiling. There was on one side the Catholic church, enormous, two big towers of bells, and across from it, the synagogue, small but dignified, topped by pagoda-like roofs covered with sheet metal. The church was built with splendor inside and under the sun it was shining like silver, like a sparkle in God's eye. Otherwise it was all wood. The church stands there sternly, the synagogue's historical enemy—those two looked at each other all the day. The church was built with splendor inside and out. Its glittering beauty displayed itself when the great portals opened. The Jewish children were afraid even to look inside.

You see, that church was the biggest thing we ever saw. From everywhere in the town you could see the towers. You could never forget about it. It was such a beautiful building, but when the great bells tolled it meant trouble for us Jews. When we heard that, we children would run home as fast as we could, back into the Jewish streets. On Sundays and Easter, those were the worst times. The processions came out from the church. The peasants were drinking all the day and night, staggering

2 **platz:** German word for place, site or location; in this sense, a town square

down the road behind those pictures of the saints they carry. Then if they came across a Jewish child or woman, it could be murder. The hatred would pour out.

You see, matters were never simple there. The pogroms were all around us. Then the soldiers on horseback would tear through the town and leave dead Jews behind. One time, we heard the big bell ring out and there was no reason for it. We were so scared we hid in the synagogue. That was probably the worst place to go, but we were small boys. All night we stayed huddling together there and heard terrible noises outside— horses, screams, shouts. We were afraid to light the lamps or stove. In the morning some men came to get us. Someone, it must have been a Pole, had warned the Jews with the bells that the soldiers were coming through. Everyone got away very quickly, hiding in the forest and in neighbors' homes. Who knows what would have happened without the warning? As it is, the soldiers tore up the Jewish streets, broke windows, threw the furniture out. We came out into the sparkling sunshine and the streets were white like a winter. Everywhere were feathers from where those Cossacks cut up our featherbeds. Dead animals also on our streets. From all this you can imagine our emotions when we walked past the great doors of the church. We would hardly throw a glance inside, even though the beauty would draw us like moths. ∾

Trinity Cathedral, Russia.

Responding to Cluster One

Who were the immigrants and why did they come?

Thinking Skill INVESTIGATING

1. For each selection listed below, tell who the immigrants were and why they decided to emigrate. A chart like the one below will help you organize your information.

Selection	Who Emigrated	Reasons for Emigrating
General Considerations		
A Slave Narrative		
Old Skibbereen		
Gold Mountain Poems		
The Pogroms Were All Around Us		

2. Rewrite "The New Colossus" in your own words. Then discuss how this poem relates to the stories of the immigrants in this cluster.

3. In your opinion, which person in this cluster (if free to do so) would be most likely to leave America and resettle in his or her homeland? Explain your answer.

4. Do you think you could ever leave your home to begin a life in a new country?

Writing Activity: Investigative Interview

To learn more about immmigration, **investigate** and record an immigrant experience in your own family or community. To do this, find a person who emigrated to the United States and who is willing to be interviewed. Here are some simple steps you can follow.

1. Schedule an interview time.
2. Prepare 5-10 questions you plan to ask. (Note that questions should require more than simple Yes/No responses.)
3. Ask the interviewee for permission to use a tape recorder if you plan to use one.
4. Transcribe, or write out, important parts of your interview to share with the class.

An Effective Interview

- records the date, time, place, purpose of the interview, and name of person interviewed
- supplies background information about the interviewee
- examines the immigrant experience with questions that begin with *who, what, when, where, how,* and *why*
- condenses information and deletes unimportant material
- can be presented using a question-and-answer format

CLUSTER TWO

What First Experiences Did Immigrants Have?
Thinking Skill ANALYZING

IMMIGRANT KIDS

RUSSELL FREEDMAN

In the years around the turn of the century, immigration to America reached an all-time high. Between 1880 and 1920, 23 million immigrants arrived in the United States. They came mainly from the countries of Europe, especially from impoverished towns and villages in southern and eastern Europe. The one thing they had in common was a fervent belief that in America, life would be better.

Most of these immigrants were poor. Somehow they managed to scrape together enough money to pay for their passage to America. Many immigrant families arrived penniless. Others had to make the journey in stages. Often the father came first, found work, and sent for his family later.

Immigrants usually crossed the Atlantic as steerage passengers. Reached by steep, slippery stairways, the steerage lay deep down in the hold of the ship. It was occupied by passengers paying the lowest fare.

Men, women, and children were packed into dark, foul-smelling compartments. They slept in narrow bunks stacked three high. They had no showers, no lounges, and no dining rooms. Food served from huge kettles was dished into dinner pails provided by the steamship company. Because steerage conditions were crowded and uncomfortable, passengers spent as much time as possible up on deck.

The voyage was an ordeal, but it was worth it. They were on their way to America.

The great majority of immigrants landed in New York City, at America's busiest port. They never forgot their first glimpse of the Statue of Liberty.

Italian immigrant family looking for lost luggage, 1905.
Photo by Lewis W. Hine.

Edward Corsi, who later became United States Commissioner of Immigration, was a ten-year-old Italian immigrant when he sailed into New York harbor in 1907:

My first impressions of the New World will always remain etched in my memory, particularly that hazy October morning when I first saw Ellis Island. The steamer *Florida,* fourteen days out of Naples, filled to capacity with 1,600 natives of Italy, had weathered one of the worst storms in our captain's memory; and glad we were, both children and grown-ups, to leave the open sea and come at last through the Narrows into the Bay.

A mother and her children arrive at Ellis Island.

My mother, my stepfather, my brother Giuseppe, and my two sisters, Liberta and Helvetia, all of us together, happy that we had come through the storm safely, clustered on the foredeck for fear of separation and looked with wonder on this miraculous land of our dreams.

Giuseppe and I held tightly to Stepfather's hands, while Liberta and Helvetia clung to Mother. Passengers all about us were crowding against the rail. Jabbered conversation, sharp cries, laughs and cheers—a steadily rising din filled the air. Mothers and fathers lifted up babies so that they too could see, off to the left, the Statue of Liberty. . . .

Finally the *Florida* veered to the left, turning northward into the Hudson River, and now the incredible buildings of lower Manhattan came very close to us.

The officers of the ship . . . went striding up and down the decks shouting orders and directions and driving the immigrants before them. Scowling and gesturing, they pushed and pulled the passengers, herding us into separate groups as though we were animals. A few moments later we came to our dock, and the long journey was over.

▲   ▲   ▲

But the journey was not yet over. Before they could be admitted to the United States, immigrants had to pass through Ellis Island, which became the nation's chief immigrant processing center in 1892. There they would be questioned and examined. Those who could not pass all the exams would be detained; some would be sent back to Europe. And so their arrival in America was filled with great anxiety. Among the immigrants, Ellis Island was known as "Heartbreak Island."

When their ship docked at a Hudson River pier, the immigrants had numbered identity tags pinned to their clothing. Then they were herded onto special ferryboats that carried them to Ellis Island. Officials hurried them along, shouting "Quick! Run! Hurry!" in half a dozen languages.

Filing into an enormous inspection hall, the immigrants formed long lines separated by iron railings that made the hall look like a great maze.

Now the examinations began. First the immigrants were examined by two doctors of the United States Health Service. One doctor looked for physical and mental abnormalities. When a case aroused suspicion, the immigrant received a chalk mark on the right shoulder for further inspection: L for lameness, H for heart, X for mental defects, and so on.

The second doctor watched for contagious and infectious diseases. He looked especially for infections of the scalp and at the eyelids for symptoms of trachoma, a blinding disease. Since trachoma caused more than half of all medical detentions, this doctor was greatly feared. He stood directly in the immigrant's path. With a swift movement, he would grab the immigrant's eyelid, pull it up, and peer beneath it. If all was well, the immigrant was passed on.

Those who failed to get past both doctors had to undergo a more thorough medical exam. The others moved on to the registration clerk, who questioned them with the aid of an interpreter: What is your name? Your nationality? Your occupation? Can you read and write? Have you ever been in prison? How much money do you have with you? Where are you going?

Some immigrants were so flustered that they could not answer. They were allowed to sit and rest and try again.

About one immigrant out of every five or six was detained for additional examinations or questioning.

The writer Angelo Pellegrini has recalled his own family's detention at Ellis Island:

> We lived there for three days—Mother and we five children, the youngest of whom was three years old. Because of the rigorous physical examination that we had to submit to, particularly of the eyes, there was this terrible anxiety that one of us might be rejected. And if one of us was, what would the rest of the family do? My sister was indeed momentarily rejected; she had been so ill and had cried so much that her eyes were absolutely bloodshot, and Mother was told, "Well, we can't let her in." But fortunately, Mother was an indomitable spirit and finally made them understand that if her child had a few hours' rest and a little bite to eat she would be all right. In the end we did get through.

▲ ▲ ▲

Most immigrants passed through Ellis Island in about one day. Carrying all their worldly possessions, they left the examination hall and waited on the dock for the ferry that would take them to Manhattan, a mile away. Some of them still faced long journeys overland before they reached their final destination. Others would head directly for the teeming immigrant neighborhoods of New York City. . . .

Immigrants still come to America. Since World War II, more than 8 million immigrants have entered the country. While this is a small number compared to the mass migrations at the turn of century, the United States continues to admit more immigrants than any other nation.

Many of today's immigrants come from countries within the Western Hemisphere, and from Asia and Africa as well as Europe. When they reach the United States, they face many of the same problems and hardships that have always confronted newcomers. And they come here for the same reason that immigrants have always come: to seek a better life for themselves and their children. ∾

Dutch children hold health inspection cards.

The four Gatzoyiannis children in 1949, just before boarding a ship for America.
The author is the young boy in front.

GOING TO AMERICA

NICHOLAS GAGE

*In 1949, at the age of twelve, Nicholas Gage left Greece with his sisters
to be united with their father in America. Their mother had been
killed by invading Communist guerrillas in their mountain village, but
her four children had escaped. Prokopi Koulisis, an acquaintance
from a neighboring village, helped watch the children on the eighteen-day
journey to America. In this selection, Nicholas remembers his first
thoughts and emotions as the ship leaves Greece—and eighteen days
later when it arrives in America.*

As the ship began to pull away, I watched the figure of my grand-
father shrinking. Suddenly he began to wave the walking stick he
always carried, carved from the branch of a cornel tree and polished to
a dark sheen by his hands. Finally it was only the frantic waving of his
stick that distinguished him from the other dots on the harborside.

. . . My fingers touched something cold and smooth, and I pulled it out
of my pocket. It was the small black stone that I had picked up outside
my house on the night of our escape, because my mother had ordered
me to throw one behind me so that I would never return to the place that
gave us so much suffering. I had kept that stone in my pocket for eight
months, and now it was time to toss it into the sea.

My mother had often told us the story of how my father, an itinerant
tinker[1] of seventeen, when he boarded the ship for America, triumphantly

---

1 **tinker:** mender of household utensils

Passport photo of the author and his sisters.

tossed over the rail the fez[2] that the Turkish occupiers of northern Greece forced men to wear in those days as a symbol of their subjugation. When the fez disappeared into the waves, she said, my father felt like a free man for the first time in his life.

Now it was my turn to throw this stone from my village into the same sea, to insure that I would never be pulled back to this land of war and famine, bombs, torture and executions. My mother had said that any one of her children who came back would receive her curse. Throwing the stone was the way to turn my back irrevocably on Greece and my face toward America, where my father waited.

But my mother's body was still in Greece, in the church only a few yards below our ruined house. They had called her the *Amerikana*[3] and all her life she had dreamed of America, but she would never leave our mountains. My sister was still somewhere behind those mountains, too, unless she was dead.

It was the only country I knew, and I loved the cruel beauty of the mountain peaks, the sound of the goats' bells in the thin air, the smell

2 **fez**: cone-shaped hat with flat top, tassel, and no brim; worn by men of Turkey and other middle Eastern countries

3 *Amerikana*: "the American one"; nickname given to the author's mother because her husband had gone to America to work

of wood smoke, and the annual transfiguration of the gray hillsides when the Judas trees and wildflowers burst into paschal colors in the spring. I wasn't sorry to be leaving Greece, but despite my mother's orders, I couldn't make myself throw that stone overboard and cut myself off from my native land forever. It was the only place I had ever felt I belonged, until the war killed my mother and washed my sisters and me away like the swells of the sea that frightened me so when I first saw its vastness.

I slipped the stone back into my pocket and turned to follow my sisters, who were descending the steel stairs into the bowels of the ship, crying out in dismay at the dizzying sway beneath their feet. . . .

▲   ▲   ▲

On the eighteenth day of our journey, I got up before dawn to put on my scratchy woolen suit, then went up to the deck, much too excited to eat breakfast. As soon as the darkness lifted and the haze burned off I saw it—two strips of land reaching out to us, the arms of America pulling us to her bosom.

The deck quickly filled as the ship approached New York harbor. My sisters gathered around me, silent at the rail, and I could feel Prokopi Koulisis' hands on my shoulders.

When I could make out details of the land, I felt an ache of disappointment. There were pockets of dingy gray snow in the hollows and a grim, metallic sky overhead. I couldn't help thinking that now, in Greece, oranges and lemons were ripening on the trees under a warm blue sky.

"The Statue!" someone cried, and there was a stampede to the other side of the ship toward the immense figure of the woman my father called Saint Freedom. She faced us, holding the torch that had welcomed millions of refugees from famine, war, poverty, and persecution, each one no doubt as frightened as I was now. Everyone started shouting and pointing, but when we drew close, the throng fell silent, as if in the presence of a miracle.

When we neared the dock, I turned toward the crowd of people waiting on land, trying to recognize the father I had never seen. I expected him to tower over the rest like a colossus,[4] so I paid no attention to a short, portly man in a stylish felt hat and gray chesterfield,[5] standing in the

4 **colossus:** huge statue
5 **chesterfield:** overcoat with velvet collar

very front of the crowd. But Prokopi Koulisis remembered my father from his visits to our village, and I felt strong arms lift me up off the deck, holding me high above the heads of the crowd like a trophy as Olga shouted, *"Patera!"*[6] The stocky man on the dock snatched his hat from his bald head and began waving it.

Twenty-five years later, when he was eighty-one years old, my father described the scene in his broken English into a tape recorder. "I was on the dock watching the boat," he began slowly. "Olga recognize me. And I wave to them. Prokopi Koulisis, he pick Nikola up and show him to me from the deck. First time I see my son. Oh, my tears! My heart broke that minute."

He paused, trying to collect himself while two small grandchildren played at his feet. "They start to come out," he went on doggedly. "I hugged him, his little arms. They was so cold. My own childrens!"

He turned toward the machine that was recording his words. "I think I have to stop now," he said apologetically, "because I'm going to cry."

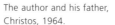

The author and his father, Christos, 1964.

6 *Patera*: father

His tearful words of remembrance, our cries of greeting across the water, the murmurs of wonder at the sight of the statue who lifts her lamp beside the golden door—all these sounds are part of the chorus of the millions who entered this harbor seeking a place where they would be safe and free. First they came from northern Europe to settle a raw new nation, then from southern Europe, at the end of the nineteenth century and the beginning of the twentieth, seeking sanctuary from pogroms[7] and famines, dictatorships, death camps and genocide.[8] Entering this place, each uttered the same hymn of thanksgiving in his own tongue.

Today that chorus has grown faint in our ears, for the old European immigrants have passed away, taking their memories with them. Their children have forgotten what it means not to be American. The new arrivals, fleeing from Asia, Latin America, and the Middle East, are still trying to find homes and jobs, to learn the language and send their children to school. They have not yet found a voice to tell their tale.

[The] story of the children of Eleni Gatzoyiannis in America is the recollection of an immigrant who arrived at midcentury, old enough to be molded by the traditions left behind but young enough to belong in this new world. The particular calamities, heartaches, and triumphs in [our story] are unique to my sisters and me, but our odyssey is as old as the nation: the arduous journey across the bridge that separates an old familiar world from a new and frightening one, to find a place for ourselves on the other side. ❧

---

7 **pogroms:** organized massacres of innocent or helpless people
8 **genocide:** the planned destruction of a group of people

THE HARDSHIPS OF
A GREENHORN

MICHAEL PUPIN

My first night under the Stars and Stripes was spent in Castle Garden.[1] It was a glorious night, I thought; no howling of the gales, no crashing of the waves, and no tumbling motion of the world beneath my feet, such as I had experienced on the immigrant ship. The feeling of being on *terra firma*[2] sank deep into my consciousness and I slept the sound sleep of a healthy youth, although my bed was a bare floor. The very early morning saw me at my breakfast, enjoying a huge bowl of hot coffee and a big chunk of bread with some butter, supplied by the Castle Garden authorities at Uncle Sam's expense. Then I started out, eager to catch a glimpse of great New York, feeling, in the words of the psalmist, "as a strong man ready to run a race."[3] An old lady sat near the gate of Castle Garden offering cakes and candies for sale. A piece of prune pie caught my eye, and no true Serb can resist the allurements of prunes. It is a national sweetmeat. I bought it, paying five cents for it, the only money I had, and then I made a bee-line across Battery Park, at the same time attending to my pie. My first bargain in America proved a failure. The prune pie was a deception; it was a prune pie filled with prune pits, and I thought of the words of my fellow passenger on the

1 **Castle Garden:** immigrant station prior to construction of Ellis Island

2 *terra firma*: Latin phrase for firm earth; solid ground

3 **"as a strong man...":** from the Bible, Psalm 19:5

Immigrants such as this young man were often referred to as "greenhorns."

AUTOBIOGRAPHY   **47**

immigrant ship who had said: "No matter who you are or what you know or what you have you will be a greenhorn[4] when you land in America." The prune-pie transaction whispered into my ear: "Michael, you are a greenhorn; this is the first experience in your life as a greenhorn. Cheer up! Get ready to serve your apprenticeship as a greenhorn before you can establish your claim to any recognition," repeating the words of my prophetic fellow passenger who had served his apprenticeship in America. No prophet ever uttered a truer word.

The old Stevens House, a white building with green window-shutters, stood at the corner of Broadway and Bowling Green. When I reached this spot and saw the busy beehive called Broadway, with thousands of telegraph-wires stretching across it like a cobweb between huge buildings, I was overawed, and wondered what it meant. Neither Budapest, nor Prague, nor Hamburg had looked anything like it. My puzzled and panicky expression and the red fez on my head must have attracted considerable attention, because suddenly I saw myself surrounded by a small crowd of boys of all sizes, jeering and laughing and pointing at my fez. They were newsboys and bootblacks,[5] who appeared to be anxious to have some fun at my expense. I was embarrassed and much provoked, but controlled my Serbian temper. Presently one of the bigger fellows walked up to me and knocked the fez off my head. I punched him on the nose and then we clinched. My wrestling experiences on the pasturelands of Idvor came to my rescue. The bully was down in a jiffy, and his chums gave a loud cheer of ringing laughter. I thought it was a signal for general attack, but they did not touch me nor interfere in any way. They acted like impartial spectators, anxious to see that the best man won. Suddenly I felt a powerful hand pulling me up by the collar, and when I looked up I saw a big official with a club in his hand and a fierce expression in his eye. He looked decidedly unfriendly, but after listening to the appeals of the newsboys and bootblacks who witnessed the fight he softened and handed me my fez. The boys who a little while before had jeered and tried to guy[6] me, evidently appealed in my behalf when the policeman interfered. They had actually become my friends. When I walked away toward Castle Garden, with my red fez proudly cocked on my head, the boys cheered. I thought to myself that the unpleasant incident was worth my while, because it taught me that I was in a country where even

4 **greenhorn:** newcomer unacquainted with customs
5 **bootblacks:** people who shine shoes
6 **guy:** make fun of or ridicule

among the street urchins there was a strong sentiment in favor of fair play even to a Serbian greenhorn. America was different from Austria-Hungary. I never forgot the lesson and never had a single reason to change my opinion.

A gentleman who had witnessed the fight joined me on my return trip to Castle Garden, and when we reached the employment bureau he offered me a job. When I learned that one of my daily duties would be to milk a cow, I refused. According to Serb traditions, milking a cow is decidedly a feminine job. Another gentleman, a Swiss foreman on a Delaware farm, offered me another job, which was to drive a team of mules and help in the work of hauling things to the field preparatory for spring planting. I accepted gladly, feeling confident that I knew all about driving animals, although I had never even seen a mule in all my experiences in Idvor. We left for Philadelphia that forenoon and caught there the early afternoon boat for Delaware City, where we arrived late in the afternoon.

As we passed through Philadelphia I asked the Swiss foreman whether that was the place where a hundred years before famous Benjamin Franklin flew his kite, and he answered that he had never heard of the gentleman, and that I must have meant William Penn. "No," said I, "because I never heard of this gentleman." "You have still to learn a thing or two about American history," said the Swiss foreman, with a superior air. "Yes, indeed," I said, "and I intend to do it as soon as I have learned a thing or two about the English language"; and I wondered whether the Swiss foreman who had never heard of Benjamin Franklin and his kite had really learned a thing or two in American history, although he had lived some fifteen years in the United States.

There were quite a number of farmers on the Delaware boat, every one of them wearing a long goatee but no mustache; such was the fashion at that time. Every one of them had the brim of his slouch hat turned down, covering his eyes completely. As they conversed they looked like wooden images; they made no gestures and I could not catch the expression of their hidden eyes; without these powerful aids to the understanding of the spoken word I could not make out a single syllable in their speech. The English language sounded to me like an inarticulate mode of speech, just as inarticulate as the joints of those imperturbable Delaware farmers. I wondered whether I should ever succeed in learning a thing or two in this most peculiar tongue. I thought of the peasants at the neighborhood gatherings in Idvor, and of their winged words, each of which found its way straight into my soul. There also appeared before my mental vision the image of Baba Batikin, with fire in his eye and a vibratory movement of his hand accompanying his stirring tales of Prince Marko. How different and how superior those peasants of Idvor appeared to me when I compared them with the farmers on that Delaware boat! "Impossible," said I, "that a Serb peasant should be so much superior to the American peasant!" Something wrong with my judgement, thought I, and I charged it to my being a greenhorn and unable to size up an American farmer.

At the boat-landing in Delaware City a farm-wagon was awaiting us, and we reached the farm at supper-time. The farm-buildings were fully a mile from the town, standing all by themselves; there was no village and there were no neighbors, and the place looked to me like a camp. There was no village life among American farmers, I was told, and I understood then why those farmers on the Delaware boat were so devoid of all animation.[7] The farm-hands were all young fellows, but considerably older than myself, and when the foreman introduced me to them, by my Christian name, I found that most of them spoke German with a Swiss accent, the same which the foreman had who brought me from New York. One of them asked me how long I had been in the country, and when I told him that I was about twenty-four hours in the country, he smiled and said that he thought so, evidently on account of the unmistakable signs of a greenhorn which he saw all over me.

The first impression of an American farm was dismal. In the mess-room, however, where supper was served, everything was neat and lovely, and the supper looked to me like a holiday feast. I became more reconciled to the American farm. The farm-hands ate much and spoke very little, and when they finished they left the dining-room without any ceremony. I was left alone, and moved my chair close to a warm stove and waited for somebody to tell me what to do next. Presently two women came in and proceeded to clear the supper-table; they spoke English and seemed to pay no attention to me. They probably thought that I was homesick and avoided disturbing me. Presently I saw a young girl, somewhat younger than myself. She pretended to be helping the women, but I soon discovered that she had another mission. Her appearance reminded me of a young Vila, a Serbian fairy, who in the old

---

7 **devoid of all animation:** lacking enthusiastic expression

Serbian ballads plays a most wonderful part. No hero ever perished through misfortune who had the good fortune to win the friendship of a Vila. Supernatural both in intelligence and in physical skill, the Vilae could always find a way out of every difficulty. I felt certain that if there ever was a Vila this young girl was one. Her luminous blue eyes, her finely chiselled features, and her graceful movements made a strange impression upon me. I imagined that she could hear the faintest sound, that she could see in the darkest night, and that, like a real Vila, she could feel not only the faintest breezes but even the thoughts of people near her. She certainly felt my thoughts. Pointing to a table in a corner of the dining-room, she directed my attention to writing-paper and ink, placed there for the convenience of farm-hands. I understood her meaning, although I did not understand her words. I spent the evening writing a letter to my mother. This was my wish, and the Vila must have read it in my face.

One of the farm-hands, a Swiss, came in after a while in order to remind me that it was bedtime and to inform me that early in the morning he would wake me up and take me to the barn, where my job would be assigned to me. He kept his word, and with lantern in hand he took me long before sunrise to the barn and introduced me to two mules which he put in my charge. I cleaned them and fed them while he watched and directed; after breakfast he showed me how to harness and hitch them up. I took my turn in the line of teams hauling manure to the fields. He warned me not to apply myself too zealously to the work of loading and unloading, until I had become gradually broken in, otherwise I should be laid up stiff as a rod. The next day I was laid up, stiffer than a rod. He was much provoked, and called me the worst "greenhorn" that he ever saw. But, thanks to the skilled and tender care of the ladies on the farm, I was at my job again two days later. My being a greenhorn appealed to their sympathy; they seemed to have the same kind of soul which I had first observed in my American friends who paid my fare from Vienna to Prague.

One of my mules gave me much trouble, and the more he worried me the more amusement he seemed to furnish to the other farm-hands, rough immigrants of foreign birth. He did not bite, nor did he kick, as some of the mules did, but he protested violently against my putting the bridle on his head. The other farm-hands had no advice to offer; they seemed to enjoy my perplexity. I soon discovered that the troublesome mule could not stand anybody touching his ears. That was his ticklish spot. I finally got around it; I never took his bridle off on working-days, but only removed the bit, so that he could eat. On Sunday mornings, however, when I had all the time I wanted, I took his bridle off, cleaned it, and put it on, and did not remove it again for another week. The foreman and the superintendent discovered my trick and approved of it, and so the farm-hands lost the amusement which they had had at my expense every morning at the harnessing hour. I noticed that they were impressed by my trick and did not address me by the name of greenhorn quite so often. They were also surprised to hear me make successful attempts to speak English. Nothing counts so much in the immigrant's bid for promotion to a grade above that of a greenhorn as the knowledge of the English language. In these efforts I received a most unexpected assistance, and for that I was much indebted to my red fez.

On every trip from the barnyard to the fields, my mules and I passed by the superintendent's quarters, and there behind the wall of neatly piled-up cord-wood I observed every now and then the golden curls of my American Vila. She cautiously watched there, just like a Serbian Vila at the edge of a forest. My red fez perched up on a high seat behind the mules obviously attracted and amused her. Whenever I caught her eye I saluted in regular Balkan fashion, and it was a salute such as she had never seen before in the State of Delaware. Her curiosity seemed to grow from day to day, and so did mine.

One evening I sat alone near the warm stove in the messroom and she came in and said: "Good evening!" I answered by repeating her greeting, but pronounced it badly. She corrected me, and, when I repeated her greeting the second time, I did much better, and she applauded my genuine effort. Then she proceeded to teach me English words for everything in the dining-room, and before that first lesson was over I knew some twenty English words and pronounced them to her satisfaction. The next day I repeated these words aloud over and over again during my trips to the fields, until I thought that even the mules knew them by heart. At the second lesson on the following evening I scored a high mark from my teacher and added twenty more words to my English vocabulary. As time went on, my vocabulary increased at a rapid rate, and my young teacher was most enthusiastic. She called me "smart," and I never forgot the word. One evening she brought in her mother, who two weeks previously had taken care of me when I was laid up from overzealous loading. At that time she could not make me understand a single word she said. This time, however, I had no difficulty, and she was greatly surprised and pleased. My first examination in English was a complete success.

At the end of the first month on the Delaware farm my confidence in the use of the English language had grown strong. During the second month I grew bold enough to join in lengthy conversations. The superintendent's wife invited me often to spend the evening with the family. My tales of Idvor, Panchevo, Budapest, Prague, Hamburg, and the immigrant ship interested them much, they said. My pronunciation and grammar amused them even more than they were willing to show. They were too polite to indulge in unrestrained laughter over my Serbian idioms.[8] During these conversations the Vila sat still and seemed to be all attention. She was all eyes and ears, and I knew that she was making mental notes of every mistake in my grammar and pronunciation. At the next lesson she would correct every one of these mistakes, and then she watched at the next family gathering to see whether I should repeat them. But I did not; my highest ambition was to show myself worthy of the title "smart" which she had given me.

One evening I was relating to the superintendent's family how I had refused the first offer of a job at Castle Garden, because I did not care to accept the daily duty of milking a cow, which, according to my Serbian notions, was purely a feminine job. I admitted that Serbian and American notions were entirely different in this particular respect, because, although over a hundred cows were milked daily on the farm, I never saw a woman in any one of the many barns, nor in the huge creamery. I confessed also that both the Vila and her mother would be entirely out of place not only in the cow-barns but even in the scrupulously clean creamery, adding that if the Vila had been obliged to attend to the cows and to the creamery, she would not have found the time to teach me English, and, therefore, I preferred the American custom. Vila's mother was highly pleased with this remark and said: "Michael, my boy, you are beginning to understand our American ways, and the sooner you drop your Serbian notions the sooner you will become an American."

She explained to me the position of the American woman as that of the educator and spiritual guide of the coming generation, emphasizing the fact that the vast majority of teachers in American primary schools

8 **idioms:** expressions unique to a particular language

were women. This information astonished and pleased me, because I knew that my mother was a better teacher than my schoolmaster, an old man with a funny nasal twang. Her suggestion, however, that I should drop my Serbian notions and become an American as soon as possible disturbed me. But I said nothing; I was a greenhorn only and did not desire to express an opinion which might clash with hers. I thought it strange, however, that she took it for granted that I wished to become an American. ∾

Yes, Your Honesty

George and Helen Waite Papashvily

Six months in America and already I was a jailbird.

Happened this way.

The weeks seemed extra long that first half year I was in New York. No holidays, no feast days, no celebrations to break up the time and then when Saturday came around I had only twelve dollars, at most fourteen dollars in my pay envelope.

The man I met in Central Park on my first day in America gave me a job in his garage like he promised. But after I was there about two months his wife's mother got sick and they closed up and moved to the country. With my poor language, wasn't easy to find another place.

I tried silk mill and after that factory where they made statues—ugly ones—from plaster. I stayed there until head artist gave me camel to cast, only looked like a cow, this camel. I was ashamed to make such a monstrosity animal so I changed shape little bit here and there to give some camel personality to it.

But when artist saw he got mad and told me how many schools he was in—London, Paris, Dresden—(just my point, no camels living in any of those places, certainly) and I'm fired again.

Then I went for house painter but somehow the boss and me didn't suit each other. Finally I met a Georgian,[1] there were only two, three of us in New York this time, who worked in a cleaning factory and he took me for his assistant. It was awful place. I dipped the clothes to take away

---

[1] **Georgian:** person from Georgia, a country (formerly a region) located southwest of Russia

spots. The gas we used came up in my head and through my throat and out my ears. My every piece of meat whole week long was spiced with that gas.

But no matter how the week went the Sundays were good because then we made all day the holiday and took ourselves in Van Cortlandt Park where there was country and trees and flowers. We could make fires and roast cubed lamb *shashliks*[2] and walk on the grass and forget the factory. For one day anyway we could enjoy to live like human beings.

From six o'clock on, every Sunday morning, subway was packed full. Russians, Syrians, Greeks, Armenians, all kinds of peoples, carrying their grampas and babys and gallon jugs and folding chairs and charcoal sacks and hammocks and samovars[3] and lunch baskets and rugs. Everyone hurrying to their regular place in the park so they could start tea and lay out the lunch, to make the day last a long, long time.

Well, this particular Sunday when all my trouble began was in the late spring. Bright blue day with a high sky and white lamb clouds. The kind of day that's for adventures.

I had my first American-bought suit on and a purple striped tie with a handkerchief to match and a real Yankee Doodle hat from straw. I felt happy and full of prance.

Five or six other fellows and me were visiting around the park. We went from family to family we knew and drank a glass of wine here, tried a piece of cake there, met an uncle just came from Buffalo, saw a new baby first time out and so on.

While we were making shortcut down a quiet path to get on other side of the park we came to a beautiful tree foaming over with white blossoms, how they call in English, dogswood.[4]

"Flowers. Flowers," one Russian fellow, name of Cyrille, said. "I gonna pick. Take bouquet to my lady friend." I don't know who he was, this fellow, he joined us some place we stopped.

"Pick! Pick!" Everybody got the idea. "Pick flowers, take a bouquet to all the lady friends."

"Why spoil a tree?" I said. "Use your brains better. If you want to make friends with a nice young lady, ask her to take a walk. Tell her you gonna show her a bouquet bigger than a house, a bouquet growing right out of

---

2 *shashliks*: meat on sticks; like "shish-ka-bobs"

3 **samovars**: urns with spigots near the bottom; used to heat and dispense water for tea

4 **dogswood**: mispronunciation of "dogwood," a flowering tree

the ground. Something interesting. That way you get a chance to be acquainted while you're walking. Maybe you know so good on the way back you can invite for ice cream."

No, no, won't listen. They have to break the tree down. Tear his arms and legs off like wolves. Jumping. Jumping. Who's gonna get the biggest branch? Makes me sick.

"Personally," I said, "I would be ashamed to give a lady flowers that I got for nothing. That I stole. I prefer better to buy. Shows more respect. Or else don't give."

All of a sudden that fellow, Cyrille, who had now the biggest bunch climbed down from the top branches and said to me, "I have to tie my shoelace. Hold my bouquet for a minute, I'll be back." So I held. In that minute a policeman was there.

"Awright. Awright," he said. "Defacing public property. Awright." He asked us our names and started writing them down on a piece of paper.

"What he does?" I asked Sergei.

"Gives us a summons."[5]

"Summons?"

5 **summons:** written command to appear in court

"We have to go in court."

"We're arrested?"

"Something like that. If we pay the fine, everything be O.K. But if we ignore, throw away the summons, they chase us; lock us up."

"What's your name, buddy?" policeman asked me.

I explained the best I can I'm not picking, I'm only holding for the other fellow.

But he doesn't believe me. "Don't argue," he said. "Don't argue or I'll run you in right now."

I explained again. "Boys will tell you," I said. "I wasn't picking."

No, he doesn't believe them neither. "Don't alibi him," he said.

I'd be sorry to be a man like that policeman, suspicious that everybody is a liar. What's the use for a person to live if he can't thrust nobody?

So he wrote a ticket for me, too, and went away. And still tying his shoe, that fellow Cyrille wasn't back yet.

"This is an awful, awful thing," I said.

"It's nothing." Sergei could laugh.

"Nothing! I lived my whole life at home and I was never in trouble. Now I'm six months in America and I'm a crook. Nothing, you think? How my father likes to hear such kind of news? Arrested. What will our village say? The first man from Kobiankari ever comes in the U.S.A.—for what? To go in prison!"

"Look," Sergei said. "You don't even have to go in court. Send the money. Plead guilty."

"But I'm not."

"You only say you are. Saves time."

"Then the policeman's right never to believe anybody. Say first, I didn't. Then, next time, change around, say I did."

"If you won't plead guilty, you'll have to go in court and have a trial."

"Then I'll go."

"Lose a day's pay."

"I lose."

"How about we find the policeman," Arkady suggested, "and try once more?"

"No use," Sergei said. "For myself I'm gonna plead guilty, but the best thing we can do for Giorgi Ivanitch, let's we go back in New York and see a fixer."

"What means vixer?" I said. "Vixer? Kind of a fox, isn't it?"

"*Ef.* Fixer. It's a man. People pays him for fixing things. He knows how to manage all kinds of permits; he fills out income tax blanks; tears up traffic tickets. Suppose you're refused a license for something, you give the Fixer money, he finds some way around to get it anyway for you."

"Still sounds like a fox."

"That's vixen," Sergei said. "Keep straight the words in your head. You get everybody mixed up. Fixers has big connections. Influences."

So we went and Fixer had big rooms to show up he's a Somebody, but the floor was imitation marbles; the stand lamps some kind of cast-metal golded over to look real and on a veneer table sets a big plated vase full with paper roses. Is plank mahogany, the panels in the wall? I felt them. Nope. Plyboard.

"If he matches his office," I told the boys, "he's not even gonna be a real man. Gonna be a dummy stuffed with straw and a victrola[6] in his mouth."

"Shut up or you'll be twice in jail."

"So what can I do for you, my boys?" Fixer came in. "In trouble?"

I showed the summons.

"Trouble with the police?" the Fixer shook his head very sad. "Trouble with the police is serious business. No doubt you're a foreigner?"

"In the U.S.A. I am, yes," I said.

"Well, give me a retaining fee. Ten dollars is customary, but I'll make you for five and we see what we can do."

I paid him the money over.

"Now let's hear."

My committee explained the whole story.

Fixer thought. Looked through his papers. Made a few notes on a pad. Thought again. "I tell you," he said finally, "only one solution. You go in court tomorrow, plead guilty, is about a two dollar fine and it's all over. I use my connections on the side to fix everything for you."

"Look," I told him, "I didn't pick flowers. So I'm not gonna say I did. Hang me in chains but nobody can make me say I did do what I didn't do."

So that ends that. No more help from the Fixer. He's mad.

Sergei suggested how about we go to see old Mr. Cohen, he was years and years in the U.S.A. Maybe he can think of something.

"Listen," Mr. Cohen said, when we told him everything. "Fixer Mixer leave alone all. Take my advices. I been a citizen for forty-seven years with full papers. President Hayes signed me in personal. Go in court.

6 **victrola**: an old-fashioned record player

When they ask you the first question say, 'Not guilty, Your Honor.' "

"Not guilty, Your Honor. What means 'Your Honor'?"

"Means the judge. All judges in U.S.A. named Your Honor."

"Not guilty, Your Honor. Then?"

"Just tell your story nice way."

"With my broken words?"

"Say the best way you can. Probably judge gonna listen and try to understand you. Of course it can happen you get a mean judge, one that's too tired to pay attention, that don't like foreigners to bother him. But very few those kind. If you get such a one, pay your fine, don't argue. But don't be disgusted with the U.S.A. Just come and tell me."

"What you gonna do?"

"Why, next time, I vote against him, naturally. We don't keep him in office no more, if he don't act nice."

So next morning I went in court. Called the other names, Igor, Arkady, Sergei, Philip. Guilty. Guilty. Guilty. All sent money to pay their fines.

Now my name. I couldn't understand a word they asked me. I was nervous. My English was running out of my head like sand through a sieve. How they told me to call a judge? Your Honorable? No. Your Highness? No, that's Russian. Your?— They were asking me something. I had to answer. I took my courage in my two hands and spoke out. "Not guilty, Your Honesty."

Courtroom went wild. Laughing and laughing. Laughing like hyenas. The judge pounded with the hammer. Bang. Bang. Bang! His face was red like a turkey's. What I done? I was sure I was going in Sing Sing and be thrown in the deepest-down dungeon.

But the judge was giving the audience hell first. "Word honesty—applied by this—cause such mirth—contempt of court."

"Young man," Now he was through with them, it be my turn. "Address the Court as Sir."

"Yes, sir."

"Did I understand you to plead not guilty?"

"Yes, sir. Not guilty."

"This officer says you and your friends were violating an ordinance, destroying a tree. Breaking the limbs."

"Yes, sir. Some was picking. I wasn't."

"Have you any proof of this?"

"No, sir. Friends were with me, but they can't come today. They all pleaded guilty, sent you a fine. Cheaper than to lose a day's pay."

"Why didn't you do that?"

"Because if I'm guilty I admit it, but if I'm not guilty, no man gonna make me say I am. Just as much a lie to say you guilty when you not as to say you innocent if you did wrong."

"Yes, that's correct. How long are you in the United States?"

"Six months."

"In court here before?"

"No, sir."

"Ever in trouble at home? Assault or kill a man?"

"Yes, sir."

"How many?"

"Hundreds. After the first year, I never counted them any more."

"Where was this?"

"In the War. I'm a sniper. It's my job to shoot all the Germans I see. Sometimes Bulgarians, too, but mostly they didn't have much interest to show themselves, poor fellows."

"I see. I mean in civil life. When you were not a soldier, not in the army. Ever hurt or strike anybody?"

"Yes, sir. Once."

"What?"

"Knocked a man's teeths out. Few."

"Why?"

"Catched him giving poisoned meat to my dog to eat."

"Understandable. Only time?"

"Yes, sir."

"Sure?"

"Yes, sir."

"Did you actually see this man," His Honesty asked the policeman, "breaking the tree?"

"No sir. Not exactly, but all the others admitted guilt and he was with them, holding a bunch of flowers."

"I believe he's a truthful man, Officer, and this time you were probably mistaken. Case dismissed."

And then His Honesty, big American judge, leaned over. And what do you think he said to me, ignorant, no speaking language, six months off a boat, greenhorn foreigner? "Young man, I like to shake hands with you."

And in front of that whole court room, he did. ✑

RESPONDING TO CLUSTER TWO

WHAT FIRST EXPERIENCES DID IMMIGRANTS HAVE?

Thinking Skill ANALYZING

1. To better understand the immigration process, use the pieces in this cluster to **analyze** the three stages of immigration: departure from homeland, the journey, and arrival in the new land. (To *analyze* means to break something into parts and study each part.) You might record details in a chart such as the one below.

Departure	Journey	Arrival

2. When Nicholas Gage leaves Greece, he remembers his mother's order to throw a small black stone overboard so that he "would never return to the place that gave us so much suffering." Why do you think he ignores that order?

3. The mother in "The Hardships of a Greenhorn" tells Michael to drop his Serbian notions and become an American as soon as possible. Do you think it is necessary for immigrants to discard their language and customs in order to be "American"?

4. In your opinion would most Americans today insist on going to court as Giorgi does in "Yes, Your Honesty" or would they just pay the fine even though they might be innocent? Explain your answer.

Writing Activity: Journal Entry

Put yourself in the place of a young person emigrating to America in the early 1900s and write a journal entry or a series of journal entries about your experience. You might want to review the chart you completed in question one above. What, for example, do you find the hardest about leaving home? What new things have you seen? What was your journey like? How do you feel as you view your new homeland for the first time?

A Typical Journal Entry

- would state the time and place of the writing
- would describe experiences and feelings
- might end with a summary or thought for the day

CLUSTER THREE

Did Immigrant Expectations Match Reality?

Thinking Skill COMPARING AND CONTRASTING

BANANAS

MICHAEL GOLD

The neighbors were talking about us. They were worrying. In the tenement[1] each woman knew what was cooking for supper in her neighbor's pot. Each knew the cares, too, that darkened a neighbor's heart.

One night a neighbor called. He kissed the *mezzuzah*[2] over the door, and wiped his feet on the burlap rags. Then he timidly entered our kitchen like an intruder.

"Good evening, Mr. Lipzin," said my mother. "Please sit down."

"Good evening," he stammered, seating himself. "It was raining to-day, and I did not sell many bananas, so I brought you some. Maybe your children like bananas."

He handed my mother a bunch of bananas, and she took them, saying: "Thanks, Mr. Lipzin."

The pot-bellied little peddler shyly fingered his beard. He had come for a purpose, but was too embarrassed to speak. Sweat appeared on his red, fat, honest face, which wind and sun had tanned. He scratched his head, and stared at us in a painful silence. Minutes passed.

"How is your health, Mr. Lipzin?" my mother asked.

"I am stronger, thanks be to God," he said bashfully. "It was only the rheumatism[3] again."

"That is good. And how is your new baby, Mr. Lipzin?"

"God be thanked, she is strong like a tiger," he said.

1 **tenement:** apartment building
2 *mezzuzah*: a small parchment scroll inscribed with verses from the Torah, placed in a holder on the wall by some Jewish families.
3 **rheumatism:** inflammation or pain in muscles or joints

He fell dumb again. He tapped his knees with his fingers, and his shoulders twitched. He was known as a silent man in the tenement; in the ten years we lived there this was the first time he had called on us.

My father fidgeted uneasily. He was about to say something to break the spell cast by the tongue-tied peddler, when Mr. Lipzin became articulate. "Excuse me, but my wife nagged me into coming here," he stammered. "She is worrying about you. Excuse me, but they say you have been out of work a long time and can find nothing to do, Mr. Gold."

"Yes, Mr. Lipzin, why should one conceal it?" said my father. "Life is dark for us now."

"*Nu,*"[4] said the little peddler, as he wiped his forehead, "so that is why my wife nagged me to see you. If there is nothing else, one can at least make a kind of living with bananas. I have peddled them, with God's help, for many years. It is a hard life, but one manages to live.

"Yes," he went on, in a mournful, hesitant sing-song, "for a few dollars one buys a stock of bananas from the wholesalers on Attorney Street. Then one rents a pushcart for ten cents a day from the pushcart stables on Orchard Street. Then one finds a street corner and stands there and the people come and buy the bananas."

"So well?" my father demanded, a hostile glare in his eyes.

The little peddler saw this, and was frightened again into incoherence.

"Excuse me, one makes a living, with God's help," he managed to say.

My father stood up and folded his arms haughtily.

"And you are suggesting, Mr. Lipzin, that I, too, should go out peddling bananas?" he asked.

The peddler sweated like a runner with embarrassment. He stood up and edged toward the door to make his escape.

"No, no, God forbid," he stammered. "Excuse me, it was my wife who nagged me to come here. No, no, Mr. Gold! Good evening to you all; may God be with you!"

He went out, mopping his fiery face with a bandanna. My father stared after him, his arms still folded in that fierce, defiant attitude.

"What a gall![5] What meddling neighbors we have! To come and tell me that I ought to peddle these accursed bananas! After my fifteen years in America, as if I were a greenhorn! I, who once owned a suspender shop, and was a foreman of house painters! What do you think of such gall, Katie?"

4 *Nu*: expression, like a sigh
5 **gall**: bitter or bold rudeness

"I don't know," said my mother quietly. "It is not disgraceful to make an honest living by peddling."

"You agree with him?" my father cried.

"No," said my mother, "but Lipzin is a good man. He came here to help you, and you insulted him."

"So you do agree with him!" my father stormed. He stamped indignantly into the bedroom, where he flung himself on the bed and smoked his pipe viciously. My mother sighed, then she and my brother and I ate some of the bananas.

▲ ▲ ▲

My proud father. He raved, cursed, worried; he held long passionate conversations with my mother.

"Must I peddle bananas, Katie? I can't do it; the disgrace would kill me!"

"Don't do it," my mother would say gently. "We can live without it."

"But where will I find work?" he would cry. "The city is locked against me! I am a man in a trap!"

"Something will happen. God has not forgotten us," said my mother.

"I will kill myself! I can't stand it! I will take the gas pipe to my nose! I refuse to be a peddler!"

"Hush, the children will hear you," said my mother.

I could hear them thrashing it out at night in the bedroom. They talked about it at the supper table, or sat by the stove in the gloomy winter afternoons, talking, talking. My father was obsessed with the thought of bananas. They became a symbol to him of defeat, of utter hopelessness. And when my mother assured him he need not become a peddler, he would turn on her and argue that it was the one way out. He was in a curious fever of mixed emotions.

Two weeks after Mr. Lipzin's visit he was in the street with a pushcart, peddling the accursed bananas.

He came back the first night, and gave my mother a dollar bill and some silver. His face was gray; he looked older by ten years; a man who had touched bottom. My mother tried to comfort him, but for days he was silent as one who has been crushed by a calamity. Hope died in him; months passed, a year passed; he was still peddling bananas.

I remember meeting him one evening with his pushcart. I had managed to sell all my papers and was coming home in the snow. It was that strange, portentous[6] hour in downtown New York when the workers are pouring homeward in the twilight. I marched among thousands of tired men and women whom the factory whistles had unyoked.[7] They flowed in rivers through the clothing factory districts, then down along the avenues to the East Side.

I met my father near Cooper Union. I recognized him, a hunched, frozen figure in an old overcoat standing by a banana cart. He looked so lonely, the tears came to my eyes. Then he saw me, and his face lit with his sad, beautiful smile—Charlie Chaplin's[8] smile.

"Ach, it's Mikey," he said. "So you have sold your papers! Come and eat a banana."

He offered me one. I refused it. I was eleven years old, but poisoned with a morbid proletarian[9] sense of responsibility. I felt it crucial that my father *sell* his bananas, not give them away. He thought I was shy, and coaxed and joked with me, and made me eat the banana. It smelled of wet straw and snow.

"You haven't sold many bananas today, pop," I said anxiously.

He shrugged his shoulders.

"What can I do? No one seems to want them."

It was true. The work crowds pushed home morosely over the pavements. The rusty sky darkened over New York buildings, the tall street lamps were lit, innumerable trucks, street cars and elevated trains clattered by. Nobody and nothing in the great city stopped for my father's bananas.

"I ought to yell," said my father dolefully. "I ought to make a big noise like other peddlers, but it makes my throat sore. Anyway, I'm ashamed of yelling, it makes me feel like a fool."

I had eaten one of his bananas. My sick conscience told me that I ought to pay for it somehow. I must remain here and help my father.

"I'll yell for you, pop," I volunteered.

"Ach, no," he said, "go home; you have worked enough today. Just tell momma I'll be late."

But I yelled and yelled. My father, standing by, spoke occasional words of praise, and said I was a wonderful yeller. Nobody else paid attention. The workers drifted past us wearily, endlessly; a defeated army wrapped

6 **portentous:** menacing or alarming
7 **unyoked:** freed as from a yoke—a collar keeping work animals together
8 **Charlie Chaplin:** silent movie actor from early 20th century
9 **proletarian:** working-class

in dreams of home. Elevated trains crashed; the Cooper Union clock burned above us; the sky grew black, the wind poured, the slush burned through our shoes. There were thousands of strange, silent figures pouring over the sidewalks in snow. None of them stopped to buy bananas. I yelled and yelled, nobody listened.

My father tried to stop me at last. "*Nu,*" he said smiling to console me, "that was wonderful yelling, Mikey. But it's plain we are unlucky today! Let's go home."

I was frantic, and almost in tears. I insisted on keeping up my desperate yells. But at last my father persuaded me to leave with him. It was after nightfall. We covered the bananas with an oilcloth[10] and started for the pushcart stable. Down Second Avenue we plodded side by side. For many blocks my father was thoughtful. Then he shook his head and sighed:

"So you see how it is, Mikey. Even at banana peddling I am a failure. What can be wrong? The bananas are good, your yelling was good, the prices are good. Yes, it is plain; I am a man without luck."

He paused to light his pipe, while I pushed the cart for him. Then he took the handles again and continued his meditations.

"Look at me," he said. "Twenty years in America, and poorer than when I came. A suspender shop I had, and it was stolen from me by a villain. A house painter foreman I became, and fell off a scaffold. Now bananas I sell, and even at that I am a failure. It is all luck." He sighed and puffed at his pipe.

"Ach, Gott, what a rich country America is! What an easy place to make one's fortune! Look at all the rich Jews! Why has it been so easy for them, so hard for me? I am just a poor little Jew without money."

"Poppa, lots of Jews have no money," I said to comfort him.

"I know it, my son," he said, "but don't be one of them. It's better to be dead in this country than not to have money. Promise me you'll be rich when you grow up, Mikey!"

"Yes, poppa."

"Ach," he said fondly, "this is my one hope now! This is all that makes me happy! I am a greenhorn, but you are an American! You will have it easier than I; you will have luck in America!"

"Yes, poppa," I said trying to smile with him. But I felt older than he; I could not share his naïve optimism; my heart sank as I remembered the past and thought of the future. ∾

---

10 **oilcloth:** oil- or paint-treated cloth used for table or shelf coverings

BEYOND THE PALE:

Jewish Immigrants in a Promised Land

RONALD TAKAKI

In Russia, Jews were required to live in the Pale of Settlement, a region stretching from the Baltic to the Black Sea. "Within this area the Czar commanded me to stay, with my father and mother and friends, and all other people like us," recalled Mary Antin, who emigrated to America in the 1890s. "We must not be found outside the Pale, because we were Jews." In their towns and villages, Jews were victims of anti-Semitic violence.

Especially dreaded were the pogroms—massacres of Jews and the destruction of their shops and synagogues. "I feel that every cobblestone in Russia is filled with Jewish blood," an immigrant bitterly remarked. "We lived then on the first floor of a small house in Kiev," remembered Golda Meir, "and I can still recall distinctly hearing about a pogrom that was to descend on us. I didn't know then, of course, what a pogrom was, but I knew it had something to do with being Jewish and with the rabble that used to surge through town, brandishing knives and huge sticks . . . and who were now going to do terrible things to me and to my family."

By the beginning of World War I, two million Jews, one-third of all the Jews in Russia and eastern Europe, including the Russian-controlled provinces of Poland, had emigrated, most of them to the United States. Stories about freedom and a better life there were "buzzing" all around them. The cry "To America!" roared like "wild-fire." America was in everybody's mouth . . . .

A tenement room in New York City, 1908.
Photo by Lewis W. Hine.

These new immigrants settled in the Lower East Side of New York City. In this vibrant immigrant community, pushcarts lined the streets, and a cacophony[1] of Yiddish voices, "a continual roar," rose from the crowds. Everywhere there were peddlers. Carrying packs or pushing carts, they knocked on doors and cajoled housewives to buy their goods. Streams of people flowed down the streets. "Suspenders, collah buttons, 'lastic, matches, hankeches—please, lady, buy," peddlers shouted. "Bandannas and tin cups at two cents, peaches at a cent a quart, damaged eggs for a song, hats for a quarter, and spectacles warranted to suit the eye . . . for thirty-five cents." In this colony, Jews resided and worked "within that small compass, meeting only people of their own nationality." One immigrant recalled that living in the Lower East Side was as though "we were still in our village in Russia."

But the Lower East Side was also different in a significant way. It was the center of the garment industry. Sewing factories filled the neighborhood, like a huge, spreading industrial beehive. On the Second Avenue elevated train, a passenger could ride half a mile through the sweater district. "Every open window of the big tenements, that [stood] like a continuous brick wall on both sides of the way, [gave] you a glimpse of one of these shops. . . . Men and women bending over their machines or ironing clothes at the window, half-naked. . . . Morning, noon, or night it [made] no difference." From block after block of sweatshops came the "whir of a thousand sewing-machines, worked at high pressure from the earliest dawn till mind and muscle [gave] out together." Family members, from the youngest to the oldest, labored in "qualmy"[2] rooms, where meals [were] cooked and clothing washed and dried besides, the livelong day."

In the sweatshops, the work was physically punishing. The section system gave the bosses power to set the pace of their workers, who sat in long rows with their "bodies bent over the machines." Each person completed an assigned task and then passed his or her part of the garment to the next worker on the line, while the foreman nagged everyone to hurry. "Most of them smoke cigarettes while they work," observed a contemporary; "beer and cheap whiskey are brought in several times a day by a peddler. Some sing Yiddish songs—while they race. . . ." But many women were forced to work silently. "We were like slaves. You couldn't pick your head up. You couldn't talk. We used to go to the bathroom. The forelady used to go after us, we shouldn't stay too long."

1 **cacophony:** harsh, clashing sounds
2 **qualmy:** stuffy

Sweatshop, New York City, ca. 1900.

The immigrants worked in disciplined, harsh, and also unsafe conditions. "We are so crowded together that there is not an inch of space,"
one woman complained. "The machines are so close together that there
is no way to escape in case of immergansie [sic]."

An emergency did happen on March 26, 1911, when a fire suddenly
exploded at the Triangle Shirtwaist Company. Eight hundred workers,
mostly young women, were trapped in the burning building. "A stream
of fire tore up through the elevator shaft and stairways to the upper
floors. Fire instantly appeared at all windows, and tongues of flames
crept higher and higher along the walls to where little groups of terrified
girls, workers, stood in confusion." Screaming, struggling, they jumped
from windows, some from the ninth floor, their bodies smashing on the
sidewalks. Unable to escape, 146 young workers—mostly Jewish and
Italian—died in the smoke and heat of the inferno. The deaths of the
many young people stirred great grief. Fifty thousand mourners marched
in a mass memorial parade in memory of their dead daughters. ∾

TEARS OF AUTUMN

YOSHIKO UCHIDA

Hana Omiya stood at the railing of the small ship that shuddered toward America in a turbulent November sea. She shivered as she pulled the folds of her silk kimono close to her throat and tightened the wool shawl about her shoulders.

She was thin and small, her dark eyes shadowed in her pale face, her black hair piled high in a pompadour[1] that seemed too heavy for so slight a woman. She clung to the moist rail and breathed the damp salt air deep into her lungs. Her body seemed leaden and lifeless, as though it were simply the vehicle transporting her soul to a strange new life, and she longed with childlike intensity to be home again in Oka Village.

She longed to see the bright persimmon[2] dotting the barren trees beside the thatched roofs, to see the fields of golden rice stretching to the mountains where only last fall she had gathered plum white mushrooms, and to see once more the maple trees lacing their flaming colors through the green pine. If only she could see a familiar face, eat a meal without retching, walk on solid ground, and stretch out at night on a *tatami*[3] mat instead of in a hard narrow bunk. She thought now of seeking the warm shelter of her bunk but could not bear to face the relentless smell of fish that penetrated the lower decks.

Why did I ever leave Japan? she wondered bitterly. Why did I ever listen to my uncle? And yet she knew it was she herself who had begun the

---

1 **pompadour:** hairstyle popular at the time of this story

2 **persimmon:** orange-red fruit

3 *tatami*: straw mat used as a floor covering and sleeping pad

A Japanese picture bride just before leaving for America, 1910.

SHORT STORY   **75**

chain of events that placed her on this heaving ship. It was she who had first planted in her uncle's mind the thought that she would make a good wife for Taro Takeda, the lonely man who had gone to America to make his fortune in Oakland, California.

It all began one day when her uncle had come to visit her mother.

"I must find a nice young bride," he had said, startling Hana with this blunt talk of marriage in her presence. She blushed and was ready to leave the room when her uncle quickly added, "My good friend Takeda has a son in America. I must find someone willing to travel to that far land."

This last remark was intended to indicate to Hana and her mother that he didn't consider this a suitable prospect for Hana, who was the youngest daughter of what once had been a fine family. Her father, until his death fifteen years ago, had been the largest landholder of the village and one of its last *samurai*.[4] They had once had many servants and field hands, but now all that was changed. Their money was gone. Hana's three older sisters had made good marriages, and the eldest remained in their home with her husband to carry on the Omiya name and perpetuate the homestead. Her other sisters had married merchants in Osaka and Nagoya and were living comfortably.

Now that Hana was twenty-one, finding a proper husband for her had taken on an urgency that produced an embarrassing secretive air over the entire matter. Usually, her mother didn't speak of it until they were lying side by side on their quilts at night. Then, under the protective cover of darkness, she would suggest one name and then another, hoping that Hana would indicate an interest in one of them.

Her uncle spoke freely of Taro Takeda only because he was so sure Hana would never consider him. "He is a conscientious, hardworking man who has been in the United States for almost ten years. He is thirty-one, operates a small shop, and rents some rooms above the shop where he lives." Her uncle rubbed his chin thoughtfully. "He could provide well for a wife," he added.

"Ah," Hana's mother said softly.

"You say he is successful in this business?" Hana's sister inquired.

"His father tells me he sells many things in his shop—clothing, stockings, needles, thread, and buttons—such things as that. He also sells bean paste, pickled radish, bean cake, and soy sauce. A wife of his would not go cold or hungry."

4 *samurai*: an aristocratic Japanese warrior or knight

They all nodded, each of them picturing this merchant in varying degrees of success and affluence. There were many Japanese emigrating to America these days, and Hana had heard of the picture brides who went with nothing more than an exchange of photographs to bind them to a strange man.

"Taro San is lonely," her uncle continued. "I want to find for him a fine young woman who is strong and brave enough to cross the ocean alone."

"It would certainly be a different kind of life," Hana's sister ventured, and for a moment, Hana thought she glimpsed a longing ordinarily concealed behind her quiet, obedient face. In that same instant, Hana knew she wanted more for herself than her sisters had in their proper, arranged, and loveless marriages. She wanted to escape the smothering strictures of life in her village. She certainly was not going to marry a farmer and spend her life working beside him planting, weeding, and harvesting in the rice paddies until her back became bent from too many years of stooping and her skin was turned to brown leather by the sun and wind. Neither did she particularly relish the idea of marrying a merchant in a big city as her two sisters had done. Since her mother objected to her going to Tokyo to seek employment as a teacher, perhaps she would consent to a flight to America for what seemed a proper and respectable marriage.

Almost before she realized what she was doing, she spoke to her uncle. "Oji San, perhaps I should go to America to make this lonely man a good wife."

"You, Hana Chan?" Her uncle observed her with startled curiosity. "You would go all alone to a foreign land so far away from your mother and family?"

"I would not allow it." Her mother spoke fiercely. Hana was her youngest and she had lavished upon her the attention and latitude that often befall the last child. How could she permit her to travel so far, even to marry the son of Takeda who was known to her brother?

But now, a notion that had seemed quite impossible a moment before was lodged in his receptive mind, and Hana's uncle grasped it with the pleasure that comes from an unexpected discovery.

"You know," he said looking at Hana, "it might be a very good life in America."

Hana felt a faint fluttering in her heart. Perhaps this lonely man in America was her means of escaping both the village and the encirclement of her family.

Her uncle spoke with increasing enthusiasm of sending Hana to become Taro's wife. And the husband of Hana's sister, who was head of their household, spoke with equal eagerness. Although he never said so, Hana guessed he would be pleased to be rid of her, the spirited younger sister who stirred up his placid life with what he considered radical ideas about life and the role of women. He often claimed that Hana had too much schooling for a girl. She had graduated from Women's High School in Kyoto, which gave her five more years of schooling than her older sister.

"It has addled her brain—all that learning from those books," he said when he tired of arguing with Hana.

A man's word carried much weight for Hana's mother. Pressed by the two men, she consulted her other daughters and their husbands. She discussed the matter carefully with her brother and asked the village priest. Finally, she agreed to an exchange of family histories and an investigation was begun into Taro Takeda's family, his education, and his health, so they would be assured there was no insanity or tuberculosis or police records concealed in his family's past. Soon Hana's uncle was devoting his energies entirely to serving as go-between for Hana's mother and Taro Takeda's father.

When at last an agreement to the marriage was almost reached, Taro wrote his first letter to Hana. It was brief and proper and gave no more clue to his character than the stiff formal portrait taken at his graduation from middle school. Hana's uncle had given her the picture with apologies from his parents, because it was the only photo they had of him and it was not a flattering likeness.

Hana hid the letter and photograph in the sleeve of her kimono and took them to the outhouse to study in private. Squinting in the dim light and trying to ignore the foul odor, she read and reread Taro's letter, trying to find the real man somewhere in the sparse unbending prose.

By the time he sent her money for her steamship tickets, she had received ten more letters, but none revealed much more of the man than the first. In none did he disclose his loneliness or his need, but Hana understood this. In fact, she would have recoiled from a man who bared his intimate thoughts to her so soon. After all, they would have a lifetime together to get to know one another.

So it was that Hana had left her family and sailed alone to America with a small hope trembling inside of her. Tomorrow, at last, the ship would dock in San Francisco and she would meet face to face the man she was soon to marry. Hana was overcome with excitement at the thought of being in America, and terrified of the meeting about to take place. What would she say to Taro Takeda when they first met, and for all the days and years after?

Hana wondered about the flat[5] above the shop. Perhaps it would be luxuriously furnished with the finest of brocades and lacquers,[6] and perhaps there would be a servant, although he had not mentioned it. She worried whether she would be able to manage on the meager English she had learned at Women's High School. The overwhelming anxiety for the day to come and the violent rolling of the ship were more than Hana could bear. Shuddering in the face of the wind, she leaned over the railing and became violently and wretchedly ill.

By five the next morning, Hana was up and dressed in her finest purple silk kimono and coat. She could not eat the bean soup and rice that appeared for breakfast and took only a few bits of the yellow pickled radish. Her bags, which had scarcely been touched since she boarded the ship, were easily packed, for all they contained were her kimonos and some of her favorite books. The large willow basket, tightly secured by a rope, remained under the bunk, untouched since her uncle had placed it there.

She had not befriended the other women in her cabin, for they had lain in their bunks for most of the voyage, too sick to be company to anyone. Each morning Hana had fled the closeness of the sleeping quarters and spent most of the day huddled in a corner of the deck, listening to the lonely songs of some Russians also travelling to an alien land.

As the ship approached land, Hana hurried up to the deck to look out at the gray expanse of ocean and sky, eager for a first glimpse of her new homeland.

"We won't be docking until almost noon," one of the deckhands told her.

Hana nodded, "I can wait," she answered, but the last hours seemed the longest.

When she set foot on American soil at last, it was not in the city of San Francisco as she had expected, but on Angel Island,[7] where all third-class passengers were taken. She spent two miserable days and nights waiting,

---

5 **flat:** an apartment

6 **brocades and lacquers:** oriental silk fabrics and glossy wood decorations

7 **Angel Island:** immigration processing center located off the coast of San Francisco, California.

as the immigrants were questioned by officials, examined for trachoma and tuberculosis,[8] and tested for hookworm by a woman who collected their stools on tin pie plates. Hana was relieved she could produce her own, not having to borrow a little from someone else, as some of the women had to do. It was a bewildering, degrading beginning, and Hana was sick with anxiety, wondering if she would ever be released.

On the third day, a Japanese messenger from San Francisco appeared with a letter for her from Taro. He had written it the day of her arrival, but it had not reached her for two days.

Taro welcomed her to America, and told her that the bearer of the letter would inform Taro when she was to be released so he could be at the pier to meet her.

The letter eased her anxiety for a while, but as soon as she was released and boarded the launch for San Francisco, new fears rose up to smother her with a feeling almost of dread.

The early morning mist had become a light chilling rain, and on the pier black umbrellas bobbed here and there, making the task of recognition even harder. Hana searched desperately for a face that resembled the photo she had studied so long and hard. Suppose he didn't come. What would she do then?

Hana took a deep breath, lifted her head and walked slowly from the launch. The moment she was on the pier, a man in a black coat, wearing a derby and carrying an umbrella, came quickly to her side. He was of slight build, not much taller than she, and his face was sallow and pale. He bowed stiffly and murmured, "You have had a long trip, Miss Omiya. I hope you are well."

Hana caught her breath. "You are Takeda San?" she asked.

He removed his hat and Hana was further startled to see that he was already turning bald.

"You are Takeda San?" she asked again. He looked older than thirty-one.

"I am afraid I no longer resemble the early photo my parents gave you. I am sorry."

Hana had not meant to begin like this. It was not going well.

"No, no," she said quickly. "It is just that I . . . that is, I am terribly nervous . . ." Hana stopped abruptly, too flustered to go on.

8 **trachoma and tuberculosis:** eye and lung diseases

"I understand," Taro said gently. "You will feel better when you meet my friends and have some tea. Mr. and Mrs. Toda are expecting you in Oakland. You will be staying with them until . . ." He couldn't bring himself to mention the marriage just yet and Hana was grateful he hadn't.

He quickly made arrangements to have her baggage sent to Oakland then led her carefully along the rain-slick pier toward the streetcar that would take them to the ferry.

Hana shuddered at the sight of another boat, and as they climbed to its upper deck she felt a queasy tightening of her stomach.

"I hope it will not rock too much," she said anxiously. "Is it many hours to your city?"

Taro laughed for the first time since their meeting, revealing the gold fillings of his teeth. "Oakland is just across the bay," he explained. "We will be there in twenty minutes."

Raising a hand to cover her mouth, Hana laughed with him and suddenly felt better. I am in America now, she thought, and this is the man I came to marry. Then she sat down carefully beside Taro, so no part of their clothing touched. ∿

Japanese picture brides detained on Angel Island, 1916.

AMERICA

STEPHEN SONDHEIM

*From their Puerto Rican perspective,
female characters from the musical*
West Side Story *contrast
American life with island life.*

ROSALIA
Puerto Rico . . .
You lovely island . . .
Island of tropical breezes.
Always the pineapples growing,
Always the coffee blossoms blowing . . .

ANITA *(mockingly)*
Puerto Rico . . .
You ugly island . . .
Island of tropic diseases.
Always the hurricanes blowing,
Always the population growing . . .
And the money owing,
And the babies crying,
And the bullets flying.
I like the island Manhattan—
Smoke on your pipe and put that in!

OTHERS *(except Rosalia)*
I like to be in America!
Okay by me in America!
Everything free in America
For a small fee in America!

Rita Moreno as Anita in the movie
West Side Story, 1961.

ROSALIA

I like the city of San Juan.[1]

ANITA

I know a boat you can get on.

ROSALIA

Hundreds of flowers in full bloom.

ANITA

Hundreds of people in each room!

ALL *(except Rosalia)*

Automobile in America,
Chromium steel in America,
Wire-spoked wheel in America,
Very big deal in America!

ROSALIA

I'll drive a Buick through San Juan.

ANITA

If there's a road you can drive on.

ROSALIA

I'll give my cousins a free ride.

ANITA

How you get all of them inside?

ALL *(except Rosalia)*

Immigrant goes to America,
Many hellos in America,
Nobody knows in America
Puerto Rico's in America!

(The girls dance around Rosalia.)

1 **San Juan:** capital of Puerto Rico

ROSALIA

I'll bring a TV to San Juan.

ANITA

If there's a current to turn on!

ROSALIA

I'll give them new washing machine.

ANITA

What have they got there to keep clean?

ALL *(except Rosalia)*

I like the shores of America!
Comfort is yours in America!
Knobs on the doors in America,
Wall-to-wall floors in America!

(They dance)

ROSALIA

When I go back to San Juan—

ANITA

When you will shut up and get gone!

ROSALIA

Ev'ryone there will give big cheer!

ANITA

Ev'ryone there will have moved here!

(More dancing)

RESPONDING TO CLUSTER THREE

DID IMMIGRANT EXPECTIONS MATCH REALITY?

Thinking Skill COMPARING/CONTRASTING

1. For each selection in this cluster, **compare and contrast** life in the homeland with the new life in America. Think of three words or phrases to describe the old life and three for the new. Is the new life better, the same, or worse?

Selection	Characteristics of Former Country	Characteristics of New Country	Same/Better/Worse?
Bananas			
Beyond the Pale			
Tears of Autumn			
America			

2. In "Bananas" a father tells his son, "It's better to be dead in this country than not to have money." Do you agree or disagree? Why?

3. "Beyond the Pale" relates the harsh living and working conditions for some immigrants. If you had the power to improve the lives of workers in turn-of-the-century sweatshops, what changes would you make?

4. In "Tears of Autumn," Hana comes to a new country to marry a virtual stranger. What is your opinion of arranged marriages vs. courtships and proposals? Compare the advantages and disadvantages of each system.

Writing Activity: Fictional Dialogue

Choose two characters from the selections you have read so far and write a fictitious conversation between the two that **compares and contrasts** their situations. Include information about each person's homeland, his or her experience in America, and what each expects in the future.

A Strong Dialogue

- presents information as a part of conversation
- reveals characters' attitudes, hopes, and fears through their words
- uses one of two formats
  1) The dialogue format in which characters' speeches are preceded by character's name:
     Rita. I am so glad to meet you.
  2) Narrative format in which characters' speeches are quoted within narrative paragraphs: "I am so glad to meet you," replied Rita nervously.

CLUSTER FOUR

What Is the Immigrant Experience Today?
Thinking Skill   EVALUATING

VON

AS TOLD TO JANET BODE

Von, a Vietnamese refugee, tells the story of his escape from his native land at the end of the 1970s. Von's father had been placed in a "re-education camp" by the Communists, undergoing inhumane treatment for months. After his release, Von's father was asked to help pilot a refugee boat to Thailand. Von had to leave his mother and sisters behind. The following excerpts relate their flight to freedom and some first experiences in America.

There were fifty-two people in a twelve-foot-long boat. We could not move. I sat with my knees in my face. I could not lie down. There were a lot of men, and a few women. There were some kids, but most of the people were in their early twenties. I was maybe eleven or twelve.

We left on a rainy night. There were military police boats out in the sea looking for the escape boats, looking for the boat people. But with the rain, they went inside. We go and go and go. One night and the next day in the evening, we went all the way down the river to the sea because my father rowed so fast. We go and go and go. We were going to Indonesia. My father knew we shouldn't go to Thailand, because there were a lot of pirates. Most of the people who went to Thailand got killed. After four days we saw a blinking light! Oh, we thought, that's an American ship! We first saw the light around two in the morning and by six we could see the boat.

The boat was all black. It was so big and it said "Thailand" on it. My father told me, "They are dangerous people." We were afraid they would attack us. They know the boat people often have money and gold. They steal the females and rape them and force them into prostitution in Thailand. They are pirates.

My father went into the kitchen and took charcoal. He put it on the women's faces. He wanted to help camouflage them in the dark. We only had one gun, a shotgun. The people were saying, "What should we do? Shoot them?"

My father said, "No, we cannot. There are so many of them. If we shoot at them, they will definitely kill us. It is better to let them rob us."

They came on board our little boat. They had knives and hammers. My father said, "Try to act cool." I was so scared, I was shaking. Even my feet were shaking. They ordered all the men to go onto their big ship. I was so small that one man took my hand, picked me up, and threw me to another man on their ship. It looked so far and the ship was rocking that I was afraid they would miss me and I would fall into the sea. They would not bother to save me.

The pirates went around our boat checking for gold. They asked for watches and rings and money and said, "If you lie, we'll throw you into the sea." Everybody gave them everything they had, all their savings for their new lives. But after that the pirates gave us food. We were all very hungry people. They took us back to our boat. We were lucky. They didn't kill us. I guess they felt sorry for us.

We were back alone on the sea and then we saw some more big, big ships. One was from Holland, another from Italy. They saw us and didn't stop! We lay there. We were so hot. Every time we saw a big ship we got so happy. They came so close that then we got afraid that we could get caught in their waves. My father always put a white flash, a message, and it said, "If you want to pick us up, we come close. If no, we stay away."

Some of the ships said, "Yes, we take you," and then when we came close, they tried to hit us to make us drown and die in the sea. My father knew they used that trick a lot. They didn't want us there, and if we died, nobody knew. So many people were coming out of Vietnam. Other countries didn't want to take any more. It's even worse today.

We go and go and go. In two weeks we saw a ship from Germany with a red cross on it. My father rowed, rowed, rowed and he came very nicely right next to the ship. The Germans took us on board their ship. They gave us food, a shower, blankets. They told us to sleep. And they asked to speak to the captain of the boat. My father, he doesn't know German but he knows French, he went and spoke French to them. They said, "Tomorrow we will take you and your people to an island, to a refugee camp."

My father said, "Oh, thank you very much."

▲   ▲   ▲

After eight months at an Indonesian refugee camp, Von and his father learned that a sponsor from America would help them start a new life. They travelled by boat and plane to Singapore, Hong Kong, and then to the United States.

▲   ▲   ▲

I looked out the window of the airplane in Alaska and I was so surprised. I tell my father, "Rice! Rice! Rice is falling from the sky!" He explained to me what is snow. From there we went to California, where we stayed in a shelter for a week. The people said, "Enjoy this, soon you will be in your new home, Detroit, and there the weather is very cold."

It was January when we came to Detroit. I said, "What a dirty city." There were a lot of newspapers flying in the air, and it was so cold. A lady met us at the airport and took us in a really strange and crazy hotel filled with new immigrants and mental people. She said, "Here is fifty dollars. I'll see you in fifteen days." We never saw her again.

At night at the hotel, the people screamed loud. They banged on the walls. We had nothing to cook. We didn't know what to eat. We didn't know what is American food. My father went out to the corner store and he got some coffee and a sandwich. Then he bought some soup and some rice to cook. He told me, "Stay inside." I said, "Why? American people very nice. They wouldn't hurt anybody." He told me, "Stay inside."

I think of South Vietnam. It is a beautiful country. I think of my mother and brothers and sisters and grandmother. I think new people to America are hungry for their countries. Governments can be so cruel.

▲   ▲   ▲

After two, three weeks, we had a phone call, a Vietnamese voice. We were excited. There were no other Vietnamese in the hotel. He said, "You will meet your sponsor. It is a rabbi and his congregation. They have found a home for you. One of the ladies speaks French, so you can talk to them."

When we meet them, the lady asks me, "Von, do you drink milk?" I'm too big to drink milk. With Vietnamese, milk is only for a baby. It is too expensive to buy.

I think, this is strange. Why does she ask me this?

"How about soda?" she says.

"Oh, yes, I love soda."

"What kind of food do you eat? Hamburger?"

I tell her, "Oh, I love hamburger." I never eat hamburger, but I'd heard of it a lot.

So they took us to our home. It was in the basement, one bedroom and one living room. The Jewish people from the temple, everybody gave a little bit. We got a TV, two beds, some furniture, a table, cups and plates and cooking things. After that the lady and the rabbi took us to a supermarket. They said, "Von, take all the food you want."

I had never seen anything like this supermarket. The lady showed me the shopping cart and what to do. The first thing I grabbed was Coca-Cola. I knew that. And bread. Then I looked around and I didn't see anything to eat. It was all frozen. I'd never seen that in Vietnam. There we had all fresh fruit and vegetables. I got some cans of food. At the refugee camp, I saw those for the first time.

The lady said, "Do you like potato chips?"

I said, "What are potato chips?"

She bought some chicken for us. My father said, "I feel so bad. They brought us here and they had to take us shopping." That afternoon, three more Jewish ladies came to the house. They showed us how to cook, how to make chicken, how to use the stove, where to put the milk and soda. They were so nice. I didn't understand a word they said, but I always smiled.

The next day they took me and my father shopping for clothes. I was so skinny and the pants were so big. They told my father and me, "You have to come to temple to meet the people." I got shoes, too. They said to my father, "Tomorrow, we will take Von to get a shot so you can put him in school."

They got my father a job as a typewriter repairman. He didn't know anything about that. He wanted to work on the ships, but they said to do that you must be a United States citizen. He said, "Okay."

I was very scared to start school after six years. I had to skip a lot of grades. Most of the students looked at me because the way I was dressing was strange. It was so cold, I wore everything I'd bought. I didn't know where anything was. I came late to every class. I was confused and I could not ask people. They told me in sign language, "Go to eat." I went into the cafeteria. There were hundreds of people.

▲   ▲   ▲

A supervisor knew I was a new student. He took me to the head of the line to get a hamburger and the other students got angry. "Why does that boy get to go first?" I told the supervisor, "I want to wait in the line. Please." He said, "Don't worry about it. Take the food."

On that day and on other days, when I had a hard problem to solve, or when I felt sad or confused, I always look back on my past. I say, "Wow, what happened in the past is even harder. This is nothing." Let's face it, this is easy here. There were no Vietnamese kids at the school, and only one Chinese boy, but he became my best friend. After a while I got along with the other students. I met a very nice black boy. He thought I was Chinese and all Chinese know karate and kung fu. He said, "I like your country's movies." I told him, "I'm Vietnamese." But he didn't know what was Vietnamese. He took me home to meet his mother and, wow, did they have a big TV. He said, "What do you want? Food?" "Yeah." He made food for me and we ate and drank soda. I didn't understand what I was seeing. I couldn't answer his questions, but we understood each other.

Later I invited him to my house. I was doing the laundry, but I didn't know how to do laundry here. In Vietnam we use a brush to scrub it, then take it outside and hang it in the wind. I washed it by hand in the bath-

Vietnamese boat people in Hong Kong refugee camp.

tub and left it to dry. Two, three days, and it was not dry! The boy went, "Von, what is this? Why don't you bring it to a laundromat?" He didn't know my family never had even seen a washing machine.

Other kids did bring some trouble to me. They talked about the way my hair looked, my clothes. When they called me "Chinese," they did it to make fun of me. They didn't call me by name. They laughed because I could not speak well. I was really upset about it, but then again I thought, so what?

I took an art class and the teacher said, "You draw whatever you like." I drew a map of Vietnam, the boat I escaped in, my family, and all the blood. One of my drawings I put in my father's bedroom and on it I wrote, "NO MORE WAR!!!"

▲ ▲ ▲

My father and I have been here for a long time now. . . . For five years we have had all the papers in order to have my mother and my brothers and my sisters come here. We have sent a letter to the United States ambassador to Thailand. We have written to the United States representative at the United Nations. We contacted our congressman and he wrote a letter. The congressman said, "Your family is qualified to come to the United States. They are at the top of the list." Still we wait and we wait and we wait. The Communist government doesn't want to give them visas.

This year on July 4th my father and I became citizens of the United States. I'm a free man! I read the Constitution. We the people are all equal. Now no one can say, if the United States someday has a problem, "You have to go back to Vietnam." I love this country. This country is my country now. I never go back.

My brothers and sisters don't have the opportunities that I do. Today it is September and I am starting university. I am a very lucky person. And when my family gets here and we are together again, we will make such a celebration! ∾

YOU ARE ONLY A BOY

MARGARET POYNTER

F rancisco had just turned seven years old when his father died. A few
months later, he also lost his mother. For almost five years, he lived
in the teeming barrio of Colonia Libertad in Tijuana, Mexico, with his aunt
and uncle and their eight children. Although he was made to feel welcome,
Francisco soon came to realize that every bit of food he took meant that
much less food in the stomachs of his cousins. As a day laborer, his uncle
sometimes made only enough to fill a pot with beans and a few chiles.
Being able to buy a chicken was a cause for celebration.

Francisco was only twelve when he and two friends decided to seek
their fortunes in *El Norte.*[1] By listening to the conversations in the plaza
and bazaars, Francisco learned that the border patrol's jeeps and cars
and helicopters were usually deployed in the area north of the soccer
field. There, on the United States side of the border, officers stood with
their binoculars trained on the *Cañon Zapata.*[2] Although Mexicans stood
as lookouts on the hilltops around the canyon to alert the immigrants to
the presence of patrol agents, more and more of the travelers were being
prevented from entering the United States.

Since so much of the border patrol's attention was concentrated on
that one section of the border, many *sin papeles*[3] were now crossing at *el
borde,*[4] an area three miles west of the soccer field.

"It is much faster there," Francisco overheard one man say. "It sometimes takes four hours getting through the canyon. At *el borde,* you can

1 *El Norte:* the North, in this case, the U.S.
2 *Cañon Zapata:* Zapata Canyon near El Paso and the Rio Grande River
3 *sin papeles:* those without papers; illegal immigrants
4 *el borde:* the border between Mexico and the U.S.

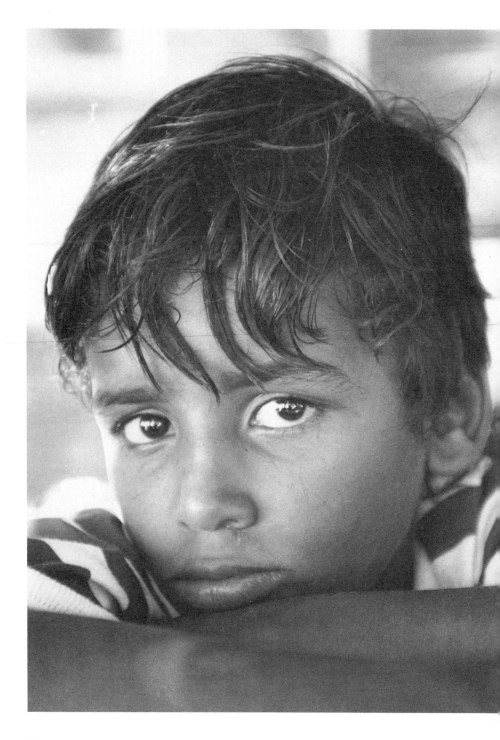

just go through the fence and there you are in San Ysidro. Then you jump into a trolley and *vamanos,*[5] you are gone."

To earn money for the trip, Francisco approached American tourists, offering to guard their cars against vandalism or to act as a guide to the bazaars and sports events in Tijuana. He also rummaged through the town's huge dump and found salvage, which he sold. Within a week, he had earned fifteen dollars.

Two days later, Francisco and his friends, each carrying a plastic grocery bag stuffed with a change of clothing, some food, a shoe-shining brush, some shoe polish, and their meager savings, were standing on the southern levee of the Tijuana River at *el borde.* They were only two of scores of men, women, and children who were waiting for dusk so they could slip through one of the many holes in the fence. As at the soccer field, vendors were selling food and drink, *coyotes*[6] were peddling their services, and sharp-eyed thieves were looking for careless victims.

The concrete levee slopes up about twenty-five feet from the fifty-four-foot wide river bottom. Some of the immigrants were waiting at the bottom of the slope, in the trickle of water that wound its way through the channel. One enterprising man had placed boards that straddled the river halfway up the slope and was charging people a forty-cent toll for the privilege of getting across the river without getting their feet wet. Francisco and his friends elected to save their money.

As the afternoon went on, border patrol vehicles drove up and down the northern levee. Evidently *la migra*[7] had decided to move their forces to this new area.

"No problem," Francisco said. "We can outwit them. And if we get caught, we'll just try again later."

When the sun went down, the officers parked their jeeps. Soon, the night's friendly darkness cloaked the movements of the people massed on the Mexican side of the border. Now, Francisco thought, now is the time. His muscles tensed as he felt the crowd press forward. He took his first steps away from the poverty of his homeland.

But what was this? The area was suddenly illuminated with a ghostly glow from lights atop a series of small towers. Confused, Francisco stopped short, as did everyone else on the levee. The border patrol was using a new and unexpected weapon in their war against illegal immigration.

5 *vamanos*: Spanish phrase meaning "we go"

6 *coyotes*: smugglers of people

7 *la migra*: immigration service officials

"There," one of Francisco's friends whispered. "Down there, outside the ring of light, we can cross. It's said that the traveling is more difficult there, but we will not be seen."

Many of the would-be immigrants had the same idea. Almost as if the light were pushing them into the shadows, they walked downstream. When Francisco reached the darkness, he stood still, afraid to move because he was experiencing a temporary night blindness after his exposure to the lights. Then, when his eyes had adjusted to the change, he pushed forward along with his friends and a group of *sin papeles*. His heart pounding from the excitement of the adventure, he slid down the side of the levee, sloshed through the water, scrambled up the other side, then slipped through the flimsy wire fence.

Stumbling in the darkness, Francisco followed closely upon the heels of the man directly in front of him. Soon, he was running along a road that previous immigrants had strewn with boulders to slow any pursuing vehicles. After crossing a wide field that was crisscrossed with deep ruts and that offered no shelter from the eyes of the border patrol, the group walked along the side of a highway that led to San Ysidro, hiding behind trees or in ditches whenever a car passed by. When they reached San Ysidro, it was a simple task to catch a bus to San Diego.

When the trio of friends had left Mexico, the plan had been for them to go to Los Angeles. Francisco, however, decided to say in San Diego, where he could be less than an hour away from his aunt and uncle and cousins. He was grateful to them for taking him in when he was orphaned. He wanted to be quickly available if any of them needed his help. In fact, his main goal in the United States, aside from his own survival, was to be able to send a little money to his relatives. He felt that his own parents would have wanted him to do that much.

On the morning after his arrival in the United States, Francisco made his way to downtown San Diego. Here, he picked a busy corner and set up his shoe-shining business.

"*Pintarlos zapatos!*" he called, waving his shoe-shining equipment at the passersby. "Shine your shoes!" The first hour he worked, he had three customers, who gave him a dollar apiece. By the end of the day, he had made fifteen dollars, more than enough to buy something to eat and to replace the shoe polish he had used. What everyone says is true, he thought. *El Norte* is indeed a wonderful place.

For two weeks, Francisco worked all day shining shoes, then after eating a hamburger or a burrito, spent the night sleeping on a bus bench or under a tree in a park. Soon, he hoped, he would be able to save enough money to rent a room and to buy some new clothes. Then he would start saving up again to send some money to his uncle. And perhaps he could buy a small transistor radio so he could listen to the music of Mexico as he waited for customers. Oh, there were so many things he could do with all the money he was making.

But then, Francisco's good luck changed to bad. One night, as he was sleeping on a picnic table in the park, rough hands shook him awake. "Give me your money," a man's voice said. Francisco didn't understand the English words, but it was clear what the robber wanted. Quickly, so as not to make the six-foot-tall man angry, Francisco handed over his savings. Just before the robber turned and ran down the path, he grabbed the bag that contained the shoe-shining equipment. "No, no," Francisco cried, but there was nothing he could do but watch his means of livelihood disappear into the shadows.

There was no more sleep for Francisco that night. He was frightened when a breeze caused the leaves of the trees to rustle. He was worried about being in a strange country with no money and no way to make a living. And he was suddenly very lonely.

Since he couldn't buy any more polish and brushes, Francisco started looking for a job. He soon found, though, that there was little work for a boy whose thirteenth birthday was still more than a month away. For over three weeks, he walked the streets of San Diego, stopping at every shop and hearing the same phrases: "We have no job openings" and "We do need some help, but you are only a boy. We need a grown-up person." Little by little, Francisco learned the English words that meant "There is nothing for you here. Go back to where you came from."

At night, Francisco stopped behind restaurants and markets to paw through their trash bins. Because of the wasteful ways of the *Americano* he managed to fill his stomach, but he was angry because he had come here to work and there was no work.

Francisco was beginning to think that he was going to have to return, defeated and disillusioned, to again take food from the mouths of his cousins.

Just a few days before his birthday, Francisco had almost finished going through the dumpster of a supermarket when he noticed an older woman looking at him. At first, her steady gaze made him slightly fearful. Could she be *la migra?* She was walking toward him. Should he run?

No, he decided. This woman wears no uniform. She wears an old black dress, much like my aunt. I will stay where I am.

"My child, you are hungry." The woman spoke in the language of Mexico. "Have you no home?"

Francisco hesitated. The woman's eyes were full of warmth, but he knew that *la migra* might use such a person to set a trap. "Oh, yes," he replied, "of course, I have a home."

The woman opened her big woven bag, took a pencil, and wrote something on a piece of paper. "Here, keep this address and telephone number," she said, handing the paper to Francisco. "If you need help, you can call upon me."

Francisco looked at the note, ashamed to admit that he had gone to school for only three years and had trouble reading.

"Follow me," the woman said. "I will show you where I live."

She knows I cannot read, Francisco thought as he walked beside her, keeping a safe distance between them. He wanted to be able to escape if this woman did turn out to be an immigration official.

They walked for six blocks, then turned a corner onto a residential street. "That's my house," the woman said, pointing to a rundown two-story wooden structure where there were two young boys sitting on the porch. "Don't forget. You come if you need help." She walked away. Francisco was once again alone, but he no longer felt as if he was friendless in this bustling foreign city.

A month passed, during which Francisco earned a few dollars doing yard work and running errands, slept on bus benches, and washed up in rest rooms. There was no one who would give him any work that lasted more than a few hours. Days elapsed between one job and another. More than once, he thought of the woman in the black dress and that large old house. When the rainy season started, and he could find no place to stay dry while he slept, he admitted defeat. Two hours later, he was knocking on the door of her house, from the open window of which came the aroma of fresh-baked bread and chili.

Francisco was welcomed into the home, which was a shelter for boys who had been found living on the street. At the time of his arrival, the woman in black, Mrs. Ortega, was caring for six other youths. At first, Francisco felt as he had when he had been living with his aunt and uncle—that he was taking food from the mouths of others, that he should be taking care of himself instead of being dependent. Mrs. Ortega soon convinced him that by going to school and helping in the upkeep of the house, he would be doing what was expected of him and would owe her nothing.

"In this country," Mrs. Ortega said, "you must know how to read and write English. Study hard, learn well, and one day, you will be able to help others who are in need. Meanwhile, I will be your mother and the other boys, your brothers." ∾

Five years later, Francisco became the first person in his family to graduate from high school. He then went to the local college to take a business course and graduated near the top of his class. It was when he applied for a job as loan counselor at a bank that an immigration official became aware of his illegal status. Mrs. Ortega interceded for Francisco, pointing out his excellent scholastic record and his ambition.

"He should be allowed to stay in the United States," she said to a judge during one of Francisco's court appearances. "He has worked so hard for so many years to make something of himself."

Currently, Francisco's case is being reviewed by a higher court, and the outlook is good for its favorable outcome. Meanwhile, Francisco is working as a box boy in a supermarket. Until he receives his permanent resident's status, he will not be able to take a job more suited to his college training.

THE TORTILLA CURTAIN

MICHAEL TEAGUE, AS TOLD TO AL SANTOLI

It was a scene more bizarre than my wildest dreams. As the first light of dawn warmed the raw desert air, thousands of Mexican men and women, in polyester and denim, light jackets and baseball caps, emerged from squalid shacks that cover the outlying hills of Ciudad Juárez. They began a rush across the shallow Rio Grande toward the Texas city of El Paso.

Some rode across the waist-high muddy river on the shoulders of human taxis. Others crowded into a flotilla[1] of inflated rubber rafts. Hungry-eyed men filled railroad bridges, waiting for a lone Border Patrol van to pass in a cloud of dust before they began scaling a massive iron gate. Smaller groups of three or four squeezed through holes in a twelve-foot wire fence called the Tortilla Curtain, then sprinted across the highway. Throughout the day and night, hundreds of others invaded freight yards, hoping to hop trains headed for Dallas, Albuquerque, Los Angeles, Denver, or Chicago—fabled cities of riches.

Between the wayfaring masses and the promised land are a handful of American border patrolmen dressed in cowboy hats and green uniforms. Their police vans can hold at most six to eight migrants for a trip to a small station house where they are booked and held for a couple of hours. When the cells fill, they are bused back to Juárez. Within minutes, they cross the river again.

In 1986, Border Patrol officers in the El Paso sector, which covers West Texas and New Mexico, apprehended 312,892 illegal aliens. At least twice that many got through.

---

1 **flotilla:** a fleet of ships or boats

El Paso is the largest American city on the two-thousand-mile U.S.-Mexican border. Crisscrossed with transcontinental railyards, it is the midway point between San Diego, on the Pacific Coast, and Houston, on the Gulf of Mexico. The border region, called La Frontera, isn't really America or Mexico but an amalgam of both cultures, languages, and economics. The majority of El Paso's five hundred thousand population are of Mexican heritage, including, in early 1987, fifty thousand illegal residents. Many have relatives just across the border. Another sixteen thousand residents of Juárez work legally in El Paso. And maybe twice that number of illegals commute across the river as laborers, maids, and farm hands up the Rio Grande Valley. Their earnings bolster the merchants of both El Paso and Juárez, who thrive on cross-border shoppers.

The U.S. Immigration Act of 1986[2] has made a modest dent in the migratory traffic, but social conditions in Mexico are ominous. In 1950, Mexico's population was around twenty-five million. In 1982, when their economy collapsed, the population had rocketed to eighty million, more than half under sixteen years old. Mexico is projecting a population of a hundred million people by the turn of the century. Inflation has been hovering at a hundred percent annually. The peso, valued at 10 to the dollar in 1980, fell to 2,500 to the dollar in early 1988. Half of all workers are unemployed or underemployed, with few making above the minimum wage of $2.85 per day. If not for three to ten million Mexicans illegally employed in the United States, who send money home to impoverished relatives, the society would be near explosion.

The overwhelming flow of migrants to El Norte, the North, has severely strained health and education systems in American cities along the border area, already one of the poorest regions in the entire country. In some employment areas, such as construction, American workers have been undercut by the migrants. And there are crime problems. Although the vast majority of migrants seek an honest living, there are some troublemakers, and drug smugglers have learned to take advantage of porous border wastelands. A congressional narcotics study found that thirty-three percent of the cocaine, forty-two percent of the heroin, and thirty-five percent of the marijuana found in the United States came through Mexico.

2 **Immigration Act of 1986:** a 1986 law that attempted to restrict legal as well as illegal immigration. Several immigration laws have been enacted since 1980, but illegal immigrants still flood into the United States.

A week before I arrived in the El Paso sector, border patrolmen made five different drug busts that netted fifteen hundred pounds of marijuana. A few months earlier, they intercepted a load of 1,997 pounds of cocaine near Las Cruces.

During my second day in El Paso, I accompanied border patrolmen on three shifts, covering a twenty-four-hour period. From the parched, barren foothills of Cristo Rey Mountain, just across the New Mexico state line, to the sandy riverbanks east of the Tortilla Curtain, I observed a phenomenal procession of illegal border crossers. Most are skilled at hovering patiently on the Mexican side to outwait a patrolman who must stay on the move to cover twenty miles of city line. An impossible task at best.

One of the officers I accompanied was Michael Teague, a seasoned veteran.

Just outside of El Paso, there's a triborder area where you can toss a stone into three different states and two countries. At this place, the only barrier that separates the U.S. and Mexico is a thin two-foot-high wire cable. It's the point where the Rio Grande stops being the international border and continues north through New Mexico, then to its mountain source in the Colorado Rockies. But from El Paso, 700 miles east to Brownsville, on the Gulf of Mexico, the river is the natural boundary between Texas and Mexico.

Here, in the El Paso sector, we have a private war all of our own. Illegal aliens are constantly sneaking across the border in droves, and a handful of border patrolmen try to catch them. I've been working in this sector long enough to tell the difference between Mexicans who are visiting along the border, having a picnic, and illegal entrants, by how they dress. If they are dressed for travel and carrying water bottles and small sacks with their belongings, like those guys on the hill . . . they plan to cross over the border right after dark.

Usually we catch young men, who are looking for work to support their families back in Mexico. But more and more we are seeing entire families. They start coming around 7:30 p.m. over the mesa[3] near Cristo Rey Mountain. A steady stream of people all night. We use our night-vision "infrared" equipment to spot a lot of illegals who would otherwise go unnoticed.

3 **mesa:** flat-topped hill

"Illegals" race for the border in broad daylight.

Sometimes border patrolmen ride horseback to patrol these hills. It's an interesting contrast—high-tech infrared machines directing cowboys on horseback. Other times we patrol in small trucks, which provide maneuverability. Before we began using night-vision equipment, aliens had an easier time coming through this area without getting caught. Now we can sit on top of a hill, spot undocumented aliens, then radio for patrol vehicles to come apprehend the groups or individuals after they enter into Texas or New Mexico.

This time of year, in late winter, the aliens try to find work on farms in the Upper Rio Grande Valley. This is the time when farm laborers start pulling weeds and preparing the ground for planting. Between New Year and June, on the northbound highways to Las Cruces, many of the aliens we apprehend are usually agricultural workers or people heading for cities farther north, like Denver or Chicago.

Perhaps our greatest concern is the trafficking of drugs tied to the smuggling of illegal aliens. Smuggling of all sorts has become big business in the border regions. Some smugglers have set up networks that may start in Central America or Cuba. We catch illegal immigrants who come from as many as eighty-five countries around the world. Even people from Eastern Europe, who are smuggled in for large fees through South America and Mexico City. Narcotics and firearms aren't always packed on aliens, but the smuggling networks being set up are more sophisticated than ever before. Since the increase of drug trafficking along the southern border, we've seen more guns and incidents of violence.

Nations like Mexico have vowed to crack down on smuggling crimes. But in some areas, international drug trade and corruption is a way of life. And with such a high demand for drugs in the U.S., it's hard to remove the magnet.

Some aliens smuggle Mexican avocados. They carry between forty and two hundred pounds of the produce on their backs. We've caught tons and tons in the past couple of years. Recently we received a letter from the head of the U.S. Agricultural Department that said many of those avocados tested positive for fruit-fly larvae or other contamination.

Some illegal people coming into this country have exotic diseases. I was surprised when I first got here—I discovered a couple of people that we apprehended had leprosy.[4]

4 **leprosy:** a deforming skin disease accompanied by loss of muscle use and eventual paralysis

It's a pretty lonesome feeling out here at night, alone or with a partner. We do get the feeling that we're outnumbered. [Laughs] I've jumped into a boxcar or a freight-train gondola, turned on my flashlight, and seen twenty-five or thirty aliens. What can I do? Surround them? I can only tell them to get off the train. If they want to fight, I'm in trouble.

That does happen from time to time but, fortunately, not very often. Most of the freight-yarders are from farther down south in Mexico. They're real docile. There have been times I've jumped off a moving train while chasing people, stepped in a hole, and fallen face down. The guy I was chasing stopped and came back to help me. He said, "Gee, did you hurt yourself? I'm sorry."

With people from the interior of Mexico—places like Durango and Zacatecas—the differences are like night and day from those who live along the border. The great majority of them are decent people coming here to look for work. Their families' economic conditions are pretty bad in Mexico. You have to sympathize with them to a point. But if you open the border wide up, you're going to invite political and social upheaval. Our job is to prevent illegal entry to our country, but we know that they're going to keep coming as long as our grass is greener. And we also know that we can't catch them all.

Mexico's population has grown from thirty million people in the early 1960s to some eighty million people today. The population is also projected to skyrocket to a hundred million by the turn of the century. Who is going to feed them and give them jobs? What's going to stop massive migration? For many of them, their only alternative is to go north and do whatever kind of labor they can find, whether that means cleaning toilets or stooping all day in the hot sun. Whatever it takes to buy a few more beans or some lettuce.

My sector chief, Mike Williams, likes to say, "The Statue of Liberty holds a torch for freedom. But she also holds a book of laws in her other hand." There're a lot of arguments from the heart and pocketbook about how illegal immigrants help this country, but there has to be a systematic order, or else we'll have anarchy.

In our sector, which stretches from the Arizona-New Mexico boundary to Sierra Blanca, Texas, we apprehended 312,000 illegals in 1986. This was a tremendous increase. For instance, in 1960, this sector arrested only 3,630 aliens; in 1970, 43,640, and in 1980, 127,428. Through 1986, all the sectors up and down the Mexican border have faced the same trend.

The message going out all over the world, not only in Mexico, is: "If you can get past the *thin green line*"—the Border Patrol—"you're home free."

After the new immigration bill passed, the number seemed to drop. That is not to say the numbers won't pick up again. Sometimes we catch the same undocumented alien twice or even three times in the same day. Because of the large volume of illegals in our sector, we voluntarily return them across the river, unless they have committed a prosecutable offense. There is no way to house each and every undocumented alien we pick up for very long. Many of them come across on a daily basis to find work, then return home to Mexico.

[We drive in the patrol truck on a dirt road along the Rio Grande, toward downtown El Paso. Across the river, in Juárez, groups of Mexican youths jeer and yell insults. Officer Teague nods his head toward them without a change in facial expression.]

You can tell they really love us Border Patrol people. [Laughs] Around here at night, it's like a game of cat-and-mouse. The aliens sneak around in the dark after they cross the river, trying to get away from us. And we sneak around trying to catch them.

We've also had agents overrun just like in San Diego. The gates of the Santa Fe Railroad bridge that extends across the river used to be welded shut, but Mexican train engineers got to where they would bust them down. Here at this point, dozens of aliens mass together throughout a twenty-four-hour period and wait for a chance to hightail it across the border. Even if a patrol unit is there.

Border Patrol officers had to sit at our end of the bridge twenty-four hours a day. In the summer, during daytime, two or three hundred aliens would mass at the bridge, just waiting for the patrolmen to go to lunch or to the bathroom.

If you didn't go, after a while the aliens would get tired of waiting. It would be like a banzai attack.[5] The aliens knew good and well that the two patrolmen weren't going to get any reinforcement. How many could we grab as they came over us? Maybe two aliens apiece. That's just a drop in the bucket when a couple hundred are rushing you.

In the 85,000 square miles that make up the El Paso sector, there are no more than six hundred agents. We are responsible for patrolling desert areas, mountains, and cities. Locally, twelve patrolmen work the

5 **banzai attack:** desperate mass attack; named for a Japanese battle tactic

line on each shift. We could use double or triple that number. Close to half our people are Hispanics. Many are from the El Paso area. And all the Border Patrol agents are fluent in Spanish. We receive several weeks of training at an academy in Glynco, Georgia, which includes language, immigration law, firearms, and physical training. The program is quite rigorous—about thirty percent of the recruits wash out.

Most of the illegal entrants in our sector come right through town. El Paso's got twelve miles along the river. Just about everything that happens, happens there. Across the border in Juárez are 1.5 million people. Like other major cities in Mexico, Juárez is growing in leaps and bounds, with a large number of transients from southern Mexico coming to the border. El Paso, its sister city, is the home of another half-million people. Across the international border, thousands of people commute every day. Many of the people from Mexico have legal work permits. Many of them return to their homes in Mexico at night. Others will stay on farms until the weekend, during the growing seasons.

When water is released from the dams up north for irrigation, the river levels get high. That means the currents are swift and quite dangerous to illegal crossers. You couldn't pay me to swim in that river—there are too many drownings. But every day and night, no matter how high it is, rain or shine, they keep coming.

The Tortilla Curtain is this multimillion-dollar boondoggle[6] of a wire fence along one stretch of the river. Some of the local Hispanic groups got riled up and compared it to the Berlin Wall and Iron Curtain. They dubbed it "the Tortilla Curtain." It hasn't much stopped aliens from crossing. They've cut big holes in it and come right through. Once I drove along the Tortilla Curtain and counted the holes that Mexicans have cut into it. From one end to the other, there were more than thirty holes. The only thing it's been useful for is to protect us from rocks thrown from the other side of the river.

The majority of the people who come across the river don't try to cause trouble. But any time you have a large number of people, a certain percentage are going to be troublemakers. Like the group of glue-heads you see hanging around the bridge area. It appears like they're just drinking Coke, but in reality they're inhaling glue fumes from the can. That's the more socially acceptable way of doing it. Some, who don't care, just spray glue or paint into an old sock or rag. They walk around with it stuffed in their face.

6 **boondoggle:** a wasteful or impractical project

They are the types you must watch, because they are unpredictable and can turn on you in a minute. The glue-heads are a large percentage of the gangs that rob aliens and other people. Some are hardened criminals. They might be armed with knives or pipes, anything that can be used as a weapon.

We've had knives and instruments like ice picks pulled on us. Patrolmen have been hurt by rocks or sucker-punched in the nose during an apprehension. We also get a lot of complaints about aliens being robbed or assaulted. At times like that I call for a backup team and try to catch the perpetrators. Sometimes we chase them down into the river, where their allies on the other riverbank, or on this side, start throwing rocks at us. Some advocates for immigrants' rights don't see that as a problem. But when you're hit upside the head with a two-pound rock, it gives you a different perspective.

Another concern is the amount of assaults and rapes that occur along the Santa Fe Railroad bridge, called the "Black Bridge," near Stanton Street. It's probably the most well-known crossing point throughout Texas. Aliens nabbed as far away as Florida or Chicago can identify this point here at the border. They call it Puente Negra.

Along the southern border from San Diego to Brownsville, there has been a tidal wave of aliens since 1982, when Mexico's economy really collapsed. Crime has also risen dramatically. Added to the problem in southern Texas is high unemployment, which varies between eleven and fourteen percent. Most economists say that the border regions have among the lowest per-capita incomes[7] in the country.

Because of the scarcity of jobs, many aliens hop freight trains to other parts of the country. We try to spend time checking trains as they roll out of El Paso. At sundown, or the evening shift, is when we catch the most aliens on trains.

My personal record was on the Fourth of July, 1985. A Santa Fe Railroad freight train was rolling out of town at eleven o'clock at night. There were 110 boxcars on this train. We pulled off ninety-one aliens. I guess it was a good thing that we caught them. The train would've needed an extra engine to get up the hill with all that extra weight. [Laughs]

Freight-yard aliens will go wherever the train is going. Many of these people know the train schedules better than we do. The Santa Fe train,

7 **per-capita incomes:** a measure of wealth based on the average income of an area

for instance, goes through small towns like Las Cruces, or agricultural areas. It ends up in the Albuquerque area, where the aliens can make connections to just about any destination.

The Southern Pacific line rolls out of there in three directions. One goes to Los Angeles and San Francisco. One goes east, toward Dallas. And one heads north, to Kansas City and Chicago—that's the most popular.

A favorite river-crossing point for freight-yarders is only a hundred yards from the tracks. They just hang loose until they see a train coming. Then they jump up and run for the overpass, where the trains are going around ten miles per hour. Many times, the aliens dash across the highway and jump onto moving trains. Just as you would imagine, some of them are injured and even killed. The chase is dangerous for patrolmen, too.

The aliens have burrowed a path under the highway that we call "the Ho Chi Minh Trail."[8] They don't actually live there. They just crawl on that trail right into the freight yard. It's a well-beaten path.

Our freight-yard apprehensions can get as high as thirteen hundred a month. Our record for total apprehensions throughout the sector is more than thirty-four thousand in a month.

We also catch undocumented aliens at El Paso Airport. Some carry false documents; others don't have any papers. Our plainsclothes agents can spot aliens by the way they dress, the way they act. Aliens wear brand-new clothes, and shoes or boots that are so new that they stick out like a sore thumb. Sometimes you can see the price tag still hanging. The aliens walk down the airport causeway and see all the people getting on an escalator, which is very rare in Mexico. They can't quite figure it out. So they stop. And they watch for a couple of minutes.

They finally think, "Okay, that looks easy enough." They walk up with suitcase in hand. They step up to the bottom of the escalator, get on it. And they go, "Whoa, Whhooa!" as they lose their balance and stumble around. The agents just sit there watching them. When the aliens finally get to the top of the escalator, an agent walks up and escorts them away.

It's not only Mexicans that we find at the airport. We get a number of illegal aliens from Europe and Central and South America. What we call OTMs—Other Than Mexicans—which includes Salvadorans, Guatemalans, Chinese, and even some Iranians. The majority get a valid visa to enter Mexico as a tourist.

8 **Ho Chi Minh Trail:** a path between North and South Vietnam used by guerrilla soldiers during the Vietnam War.

They may fly from their native countries into Mexico City, then travel north by bus, train, or by air to Juárez. We catch them coming across the river or at the airport. The majority are assisted by professional alien smugglers, at a stiff price. If we catch a Yugoslav smuggling other Yugos, chances are they met in Europe. If we have a Mexican smuggling Yugos, they probably met in Mexico City or somewhere closer to the border. The smuggling of aliens and narcotics is a full-time profession.

Very few of the Europeans we catch speak English. We use volunteer translators. The University of Texas has been a big help with people from Korea and other nationalities that are outside of our language capabilities.

Every time we catch someone from an East Bloc nation, we advise the FBI. A few years back we heard about some people who were trained in Mexico for some type of anti-U.S. terrorist operation. We never caught anyone related to it; nor were there any incidents. But it's a very real possibility—the idea of Soviets, Cubans, or Libyans coming here to perform some act of espionage or terrorism. If they were to get across this border, it would be difficult to catch them. Or, if we apprehend them and they are Hispanic, and claim to be Mexican, we would just send them back across the river—they could try again.

We're finding illegal entrants from the People's Republic of China, Korea, Punjab in India . . . a whole variety of countries. It's not hysteria when those of us who deal with this every day say, "Look, people, there is a problem. And it's across the country, not only on this border."

People have a tendency to be very opinionated about the illegal immigration problem, from "Stop them totally at the river" to "Just let them all in." Until you've really had a bird's-eye view of what goes on at border areas, it's hard to be objective.

The new immigration bill has made a dent in the flow of illegals. But it's still too early to tell just how much of an impact will be made when it's all said and done. From all indications, the legalization of qualified residents, agricultural provisions, and employer sanctions of the new bill are a step in the right direction. The new bill isn't designed to solve Mexico's massive economic troubles, so it can't be considered a "magic wand." With 1.5 million people in Juárez, many living without running water or electricity, folks will continue to cross the river. ∾

Between Two Worlds

Patricia Smith

Amira Masari, 16, has never slept over at a friend's house. When she was in the sixth grade, her father wouldn't let her go on an overnight school trip because he believes a girl shouldn't spend a night outside her parents' house before marriage. When the phone rings, she races to answer it. If it's a boy, she talks in a whisper. While her friends laugh and flirt during lunch in the school cafeteria, Amira worries that her father might come by and catch her talking to the boys at her table.

Amira comes from a devout Muslim immigrant family. Born in Egypt, she has lived in New York City since she was 6. And like many young immigrants, Amira finds herself being pulled between two worlds—the traditional one of her parents and the new one of her adopted country.

As immigration to the United States from countries with very different cultural traditions increases, a growing number of young people find themselves walking this cultural tightrope. The balancing act is especially difficult for Muslim girls. Many of America's growing number of Arab immigrants come from traditional Muslim societies that define the role of women and men very differently than the U.S. does. Many immigrant Muslim parents, who often have strict conservative values and rules of behavior, are very protective of their daughters, who they fear may be wrongly influenced by American culture. (They are so protective, in fact, that two women interviewed for this story, "Amira" and "Sahar," asked us not to use their real names or their photographs.)

"American society has a different model of what it is to be a woman and what is expected of women than the society many Muslim parents come from," says Yvonne Haddad, a professor of Islamic history at the University

Muslim schoolgirls, Morton Grove, Illinois.

of Massachusetts. "Daughters internalize what parents teach, but that often doesn't work in America. It's not what's expected of them here."

Sahar Ahmed, 15, is a shy ninth-grader from Brooklyn, New York, who dreams of going to college and becoming a doctor. Sahar came to the U.S. from Egypt with her family six years ago. The oldest of three girls, she says her parents are so worried about her getting into trouble that she is hardly allowed to do anything except go to school. Every afternoon, her mother, who works in her father's hair salon, calls 15 minutes after school is out to make sure Sahar is safely at home. "She's afraid of my growing up here," says Sahar, "and that I might get in trouble."

Sahar goes to a coed school. But the idea of teenage boys and girls being friends is alarming to her parents, who come from a country where girls and boys don't mingle and don't date. Hanging out after school? Not allowed. A summer job? Too risky.

Last summer, Sahar wanted a job so she could get out of her family's apartment a few hours a day. Her father adamantly refused. "He's afraid men would come into the store, and maybe even touch her," says Sahar's mother, Magda.

Birthday parties are also forbidden. "Maybe it's not only girls, or maybe there's drink there," Magda explains. "You can't trust everybody, and it's very important that she be a virgin when she marries."

Islam forbids drinking alcohol and premarital sex, and family honor is cherished in Arab countries. A girl's being seen with a boy could mar a family's reputation, so many parents feel they cannot be too careful in keeping their daughters away from boys.

Mona Zaki, 22, of Houston, Texas, says her Egyptian immigrant parents are more lenient than many Muslims. But she is still troubled coping with sexuality. "Now that I'm older, the problem is keeping my relationships away from premarital sex," she says. "My older brothers don't have this problem. One has been living with his girlfriend for a year. The other just does what he wants."

Amira Masari, the oldest of six children, generally supports her parents' values. She doesn't drink or smoke, like many of her classmates. "It's wrong," she says, "because God said so, and so did my parents." When her family rents a video, her dad fast-forwards through the kissing scenes. And going to the movies is out of the question.

"Other than the movie, bad stuff can happen in a movie theater," she says, "like 'making out.' I'm not supposed to be around that. My parents think I might be influenced to do that too."

Amira doesn't cover her hair with a veil as her mother does, but she wears conservative clothes because Islam requires women to dress modestly. Short skirts and strapless dresses are no-no's. Amira says she wouldn't feel comfortable wearing them anyway. A few months ago, she went shopping for a formal dress to wear to a sweet-16 party. She searched the mall for something modest and finally settled on a floor-length brown dress with long sleeves. But the dress had an open back, so Amira wore a blouse over it.

"At the party, all my friends were saying, 'Take it off!'" she says. "But personally, I wouldn't feel comfortable standing around like that. I took the blouse off for a minute, but then I put it back on. I was like, 'This is impossible. I can't sit around like this.' Everyone else seemed perfectly fine wearing bare [backed] dresses, but I couldn't."

Whether the discussion is clothes, movies, or parties, the issue for many immigrant girls usually boils down to sex. Girls like Amira and Sahar have a tough time navigating American society because their parents' attitudes about sex clash with what the girls see around them. "They don't let us do all these things because they're afraid of sex," Amira says of her parents. But, she adds, "premarital sex is wrong. I would never do it."

Last year, Amira went back to Egypt for a visit and found that she didn't really belong there, either. "I felt like an outcast because I'd say and do things the other girls wouldn't," she says.

So despite the difficulties, Amira says that the openness of American society can work to her benefit.

"Here, if I'm *not* doing something because I believe it's morally or religiously wrong, it doesn't really matter," she says. "There are a lot of American girls who won't go out with guys. Here, it's OK that I'm different." ⮑

TIRES STACKED IN THE HALLWAYS OF CIVILIZATION

Chelsea, Massachusetts

MARTIN ESPADA

"Yes, Your Honor, there are rodents,"
said the landlord to the judge,
"but I let the tenant
have a cat. Besides,
he stacks his tires
in the hallway."

The tenant confessed
in stuttering English:
"Yes, Your Honor,
I am from El Salvador,[1]
and I put my tires
in the hallway."

The judge puffed up
his robes
like a black bird
shaking off rain:
"Tires out of the hallway!
You don't live in a jungle
anymore. This
is a civilized country."

So the defendant was ordered
to remove his tires
from the hallways of civilization,
and allowed to keep the cat.

1 **El Salvador:** Central American country

AMIR

PAUL FLEISCHMAN

In India we have many vast cities, just as in America. There, too, you are one among millions. But there at least you know your neighbors. Here, one cannot say that. The object in America is to avoid contact, to treat all as foes unless they're known to be friends. Here you have a million crabs living in a million crevices.

When I saw the garden for the first time, so green among the dark brick buildings, I thought back to my parents' Persian rug. It showed climbing vines, rivers and waterfalls, grapes, flower beds, singing birds, everything a desert dweller might dream of. Those rugs were indeed portable gardens. In the summers in Delhi, so very hot, my sisters and I would lie upon it and try to press ourselves into its world. The garden's green was as soothing to the eye as the deep blue of that rug. I'm aware of color—I manage a fabric store. But the garden's greatest benefit, I feel, was not relief to the eyes, but to make the eyes see our neighbors.

I grew eggplants, onions, carrots, and cauliflower. When the eggplants appeared in August they were pale purple, a strange and eerie shade. When my wife would bring our little son, he was forever wanting to pick them. There was nothing else in the garden with that color. Very many people came over to ask about them and talk to me. I recognized a few from the neighborhood. Not one had spoken to me before—and now how friendly they turned out to be. The eggplants gave them an excuse for breaking the rules and starting a conversation. How happy they seemed to have found this excuse, to let their natural friendliness out.

Those conversations tied us together. In the middle of summer some-one dumped a load of tires on the garden at night, as if it were still filled with trash. A man's four rows of young corn were crushed. In an hour, we had all the tires by the curb. We were used to helping each other by then. A few weeks later, early in the evening a woman screamed, down the block from the garden. A man with a knife had taken her purse. Three men from the garden ran after him. I was surprised that I was one of them. Even more surprising, we caught him. Royce held the man to a wall with his pitchfork until the police arrived. I asked the others. Not one of us had ever chased a criminal before. And most likely we wouldn't have except near the garden. There, you felt part of a community.

I came to the United States in 1980. Cleveland is a city of immigrants. The Poles are especially well known here. I'd always heard that the Polish men were tough steelworkers and that the women cooked lots of cabbage. But I'd never known one—until the garden. She was an old woman whose space bordered mine. She had a seven-block walk to the garden, the same route I took. We spoke quite often. We both planted carrots. When her hundreds of seedlings came up in a row, I was very surprised that she did not thin them—pulling out all but one healthy-looking plant each few inches, to give them room to grow. I asked her. She looked down at them and said she knew she ought to do it, but that this task reminded her too closely of her concentration camp, where the prisoners were inspected each morning and divided into two lines—the healthy to live and the others to die. Her father, an orchestra violinist, had spoken out against the Germans, which had caused her family's arrest. When I heard her words, I realized how useless was all that I'd heard about Poles, how much richness it hid, like the worthless shell around an almond. I still do not know, or care, whether she cooks cabbage.

The garden found this out with Royce. He was young and black. He looked rather dangerous. People watched him and seemed to be relieved when he left the garden. Then he began spending more time there. We found out that he had a stutter. Then that he had two sisters, that he liked the cats that roamed the garden, and that he worked very well with his hands. Soon all the mothers were trying to feed him. How very strange it was to watch people who would have crossed the street if they'd seen him coming a few weeks before, now giving him vegetables, more than he could eat. In return, he watered for people who were sick and fixed fences and made other repairs. He might weed your garden or use the bricks from the building that was torn down up the block to make you a brick path between your rows. He always pretended he hadn't done it. It was always a surprise. One felt honored to be chosen. He was trusted and liked—and famous, after his exploit with the pitchfork. He was not a black teenage boy. He was Royce.

In September he and a Mexican man collected many bricks from up the street and built a big barbecue. I was in the garden on Saturday when the Mexican family drove up in a truck with a dead pig in the back. They built a fire, put a heavy metal spit through the pig, and began to roast it. A bit later their friends began arriving. One brought a guitar, another played violin. They filled a folding table with food. Perhaps it was one of their birthdays, or perhaps no reason was needed for the party. It was beautiful weather, sunny but not hot. Fall was just beginning and the garden was changing from green to brown. Those of us who had come to work felt the party's spirit enter us. The smell of the roasting pig drifted out and called to everyone, gardeners or not. Soon the entire garden was filled.

It was a harvest festival, like those in India, though no one had planned it to be. People brought food and drinks and drums. I went home to get my wife and son. Watermelons from the garden were sliced open. The gardeners proudly showed off what they'd grown. We traded harvests, as we often did. And we gave food away, as we often did also—even I, a businessman, trained to give away nothing, to always make a profit. The garden provided many excuses for breaking that particular rule.

Many people spoke to me that day. Several asked where I was from. I wondered if they knew as little about Indians as I had known about Poles. One old woman, Italian I believe, said she'd admired my eggplants for weeks and told me how happy she was to meet me. She praised them and told me how to cook them and asked all about my family. But something bothered me. Then I remembered. A year before she'd claimed that she'd received the wrong change in my store. I was called out to the register. She'd gotten quite angry and called me—despite her own accent—a dirty foreigner. Now that we were so friendly with each other I dared to remind her of this. Her eyes became huge. She apologized to me over and over again. She kept saying, "Back then, I didn't know it was *you* . . ." ❧

RESPONDING TO CLUSTER FOUR

WHAT IS THE IMMIGRANT EXPERIENCE TODAY?
Thinking Skill EVALUATING

1. Use a Venn diagram like the one below to **evaluate** changes in the immigrant experience. In the left circle, write descriptive words and phrases about someone in the first three clusters. In the right circle write information about someone from this cluster. In the overlapping area of the two circles, write some words or phrases that apply to both people. Repeat this exercise with two more people from the book.

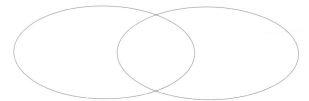

2. "The Tortilla Curtain" provides information about the continuing influx of illegal immigrants through Mexico into the United States. If you had the power to change immigration laws in this country, what three ideas would you propose to solve the problems the border guard mentions?

3. Think about Amira in "Between Two Worlds" and the main character in "Amir." **Evaluate**, or judge, how much of the old culture or language you feel these immigrants can keep and still be a part of the American culture.

4. In your opinion, what is the **theme** or main idea of the story "Amir"?

Writing Activity: Performance Evaluation

Most employees receive regular performance reviews in which a supervisor **evaluates** the strengths and weaknesses of their work. Choose either the border guard from "The Tortilla Curtain" or the judge from "Tires Stacked in the Hallways of Civilization" and prepare a written **evaluation** covering each of the following areas: attitude toward immigrants, manner of dealing with people, and overall grade from 'A' (star performer) to 'E' (dismissal recommended). Base your review on information from the selection, but use your imagination to fill in any necessary details.

A Performance Evaluation

- identifies criteria and qualities upon which the worker will be judged
- assesses both strengths and weaknesses
- gives an overall grade or rating
- suggests areas for improvement or goals to be achieved before the next evaluation period

CLUSTER FIVE

Thinking on Your Own
Thinking Skill SYNTHESIZING

THE MELTING POT BUBBLES IN REGO PARK

WILLIAM E. GEIST

Roll call, the teachers agree, is the most difficult part of the day: Ho Suk Ping He, Yana Katzap, Tkkun Amongi, Azaria Badebr, Rotcheild Boruhov, Eduardo Yun.

Eduardo Yun? Sure, the Portuguese-speaking Korean boy who immigrated from Brazil. His adjustment to America has been eased by the presence of other Portuguese-speaking Koreans from Brazil—one of whom also speaks Hebrew—who are enrolled at Stephen A. Halsey Junior High School, a polyglot[1] school in Rego Park, Queens.

"Even when you get their names right," the principal, Domenick Uzzi, said, "some are from countries where they put first names last, last name first. It's impossible."

Nicknames are popular. Chin Sheng Chu said, "Call me George." Some students pick an American name they like and then, to add to the confusion, switch names when they tire of the old ones.

"We've got everything imaginable, and unimaginable, here," said Mr. Uzzi, who said his job was simpler when the neighborhood and the school were pretty much made up of middle- or upper-middle-class Jewish students. That was before a Chinese man bought the luncheonette and learned how to make egg creams and before waves of immigrants from throughout the world began settling in the neighborhood.

1 **polyglot:** having many languages represented

This is not a testing ground, nor is Halsey a special project like the United Nations School. This is real life in New York, once again a city of immigrants. There are more foreign-born city residents now than at any time since 1930, with almost one in three being foreign born.

"New kids walk in every day," Mr. Uzzi said. "We had a couple of kids from Haiti register yesterday, which may have something to do with Duvalier's overthrow. We always know when and where there's trouble in the world. We have Nicaraguans coming in now. We expect to see some Libyan kids soon.

"The diversity can be annoying," Mr. Uzzi said. "We pair Chinese kids, and one turns out to be Mandarin and the other Cantonese, or two Russians, and one is Georgian and the other Ukrainian."

Recently, the school counted thirty-four different languages and dialects—Persian, Hindi, Gujarati, Spanish, Portuguese, Cantonese, Mandarin, Greek, Japanese, Korean and Russian, to name a few—spoken at Halsey. The number of countries represented at the school? Don't ask.

The language survey did not include those languages contrived by students to communicate. An Indian student, Chettan Patel, said he spoke five languages, two of them of his own invention. One student is proud to say that he knows one four-letter profanity in twenty-five languages.

"Cultural exchange," Mr. Uzzi commented, "it's great."

"You can discuss the Vietnam War and have kids whose fathers fought on opposite sides," said Jim Perine, a teacher.

Teachers believe the students learn tolerance. "Kids this age call each other 'fatso,' 'retard' and 'pizza face,'" Mr. Uzzi said, "I admit. But we never have fights over remarks about nationalities."

"Never a dull moment," said Irene Clarke, a teacher. New students, according to teachers, arrive asking if the school has a jai alai team, if there is a place in the school band for a sitar player or if poori bread and envueltos de maiz could be added to the school lunch menu.

Mr. Uzzi finally won a protracted battle with city dietitians and federal officials in Washington for dispensation from the rule that there must be a meat course in every cafeteria lunch. Some of the Indian students were not eating anything, because there was meat on all the plates.

For all the diversity, the school, at 102nd Street and 64th Avenue, does not appear any different from other schools, except maybe a bit cleaner and more orderly.

There is not a sari or sarong among them. "I think they issue these kids designer sweatshirts and jeans and expensive sneakers at Kennedy

Airport," a teacher, Carol Davidson, said. "They are all in a mad rush to be totally American."

Her students said they had come from schools where teachers meted out stern punishment, usually with a rod or stick. Some of the Halsey teachers concede they are slow to tell students they cannot hit them with sticks here.

"Our principal cut our hair if it was below our ears," a girl from Korea said.

"You couldn't even wear a watch in Russia," a girl from the Soviet Union said.

"Gross!" commented a girl from Queens.

Teachers said they were amazed at how quickly most of the students learned English and how quickly they adjusted. "Eileen Chang came in from Taiwan as a seventh grader and couldn't speak a word of English," one teacher said, "and graduated as valedictorian from ninth grade."

The word is out among students that the Asians catch on quickly, and one student from Guyana described them as "death" in math. "When you look around and see a lot of them in your math class," she said, "all you can do is try to transfer."

Mrs. Davidson said that Halsey students could be picked out by translation dictionaries in their hip pockets and by the new trend to electronic vest-pocket translators.

"It's nice sometimes," a student from Yugoslavia said, "being in a country where your parents can't read your report card."

Teachers said they found the mix stimulating and energizing, if sometimes confusing. "It offers teachers great rewards," Ms. Clarke said. "The students want to learn, and you can watch their progress."

She said the teachers had recently discussed an enticing help-wanted advertisement for teaching jobs in a wealthy suburb. "We agreed we could never go to a place that dull," she said.

"It's true that these students try very hard," said Sara Tsinberg, a counselor and recent immigrant. But, she added, there is a tendency to stereotype them as a quaint group of happy toilers.

"We have students ranging from the children of ambassadors to children of the unemployable," she said. "They all struggle, but not all succeed."

The final bell rang, and the students filled the hallways, yelling and laughing, before pouring out the front door past an old wood desk. On it were names carved in the traditional fashion: Takiyaki, Carlos, Trikona, Shreeti. ☙

LOOKING NORTH

ROBERTO SURO

At 10:30 p.m. on the night of August 18, 1994, Attorney General Janet Reno strode into the White House press room and in her practiced monotone announced new measures to halt the thousands of Cubans who were launching themselves into the Florida Straits aboard flimsy rafts every day that summer. The television pictures of navy ships rescuing water-weary hordes excited fears among many Americans that the United States no longer exercised the sovereign right to determine who could enter the country. As the number of rafters grew, so did the public's anxiety. Rather than be labeled a weakling on immigration, Clinton sent Reno before the cameras to declare that henceforth Cuban rafters picked up at sea would be detained at the Guantánamo Bay naval base until they could be sent home. Once regarded as the heroic victims of Fidel Castro's tyranny, the Cubans were now to be treated as just so many illegal aliens. Instead of receiving a generous welcome, they would end up behind barbed wire. This was more than an emergency plan. Unceremoniously and in the dark of night, Reno had reversed long-standing policies that embraced and celebrated people who risked their lives to escape communism. If Cubans could be shut out, then anyone could be rejected. The United States was closing its doors, and most Americans applauded.

Almost forty-eight hours later, on a beach about fifteen miles west of Havana, six men and two women, all in their late twenties or early thirties, carried a raft down to the water in the dark. White House pronouncements did not matter to them. They were committed to their journey.

They set the craft down on the sand and began their good-byes to several relatives and friends. The raft was made of three truck-tire inner tubes sandwiched between two thin pieces of plywood. By the light of a match, a man with a thick beard inspected the purple plastic cords that held it all together.

It was a ridiculous vessel, but thousands of people were setting out those days in similar craft. Some people washed back up on the beach, sunburned, exhausted, and vomiting. Sometimes rafts washed up empty. These travelers were not people of the sea. They readily admitted they knew nothing of currents and winds, but that did not matter to them, either.

The bearded man pulled the purple cords and nodded, satisfied. The raft was ready. He could care less about the U.S. flotilla and the new policies designed to halt his voyage north. Pointing his arm out to sea, he said in Spanish with loud bravado, "Florida is there and Florida is where we are going. The Americans will not keep us away."

For a moment, the bearded man stared to the north as if there was something to see other than the blackness. He knew what was there. He knew what he wanted to see: the lights of Miami glowing like the dawn. He had heard from friends and relatives who had gone before him about what lay across the water. He had seen the medicine, the T-shirts, and the bottles of shampoo that people sent back from that place. He had seen pictures of the food and the houses and the cars. Although the lure of the north was clear, the man on the beach was not happy to leave the island of flowering red jacarandas and ancient ceiba trees. Like all the other travelers that night, he was being pushed out by a life that had become intolerable in too many ways. As much as he desired his destination, the only certainty was his need to leave the one place he had ever known.

According to the inscription on the Statue of Liberty, immigrants are the "tired . . . poor . . . huddled masses yearning to breathe free, the wretched refuse of your teeming shore . . . the homeless, tempest-tossed." Unfortunately, those words did not apply when Emma Lazarus wrote them in 1883, and they are even less accurate today. The tempest-tossed were, and still are, just that. They are at the mercy of forces beyond their control. That describes most people. It is the others, the ones battling the storms, who end up taking trips. Over the centuries, immigration has reflected a continuity in human behavior, but it has always been an exception to the rule. Most people look around, see defeated expectations, and adjust. A few decide to move, undaunted by the tempests.

The bearded man would have preferred to stay in Cuba if it could be the place he wanted it to be. Like the others preparing to leave that night, he was an anxious but unwilling traveler. He buried the pain of departure and embraced the uncertain journey.

All along the Cuban coast that night, people waded into the sea. In Mexican mountain villages and city apartment buildings, in Guatemala and Colombia, all across the hemisphere, there were thousands of travelers that night, all heading north. Motives blurred with the motion.

Politics forced them to go. Their pocketbooks drove them. They had family and friends in the United States who pulled at them. They sought the freedom that comes with movement. They desired the liberating moment of reinvention. They also knew the anxious desire of wanting to join in something that thousands of others had already enjoyed. All that overwhelmed the pain of leaving.

The bearded man's wife, dressed in shorts and a short-sleeved polka-dot shirt, sat on the raft and did not take part in the exultant farewells. Her hands were shaking when she tried to light a cigarette. Her husband had to take the matches and help her.

Cubans leaving Guantanamo Bay for the U.S. 1994.

"Don't worry. By dawn, we will be out with the Americans and they will find us," he said, but the woman kept shaking. Overhead, a full moon cast pale light through gauzy clouds. The wind was warm and moist and steady. In the distance, a squall lit the sky with lightning.

The woman held herself and shivered, even though it was not the least bit cold. Asked why she was leaving if she was so afraid, she said, "If I was not meant to die tonight, I won't. Death on land, death on sea—it's the same. I must go."

The dream of bright lights draws people north. Their homelands push them out. The bold set out on journeys, as they always have before. Laws and barbed wire do not deter the most determined. Not even the danger of death stops the boldest.

The woman and her husband and the other travelers climbed onto the raft, and several of their companions waded into the water to help them push off. The men started rowing. Beyond them, there was nothing but darkness and the sound of waves. ∾

HUDDLED MASSES

MICHAEL SATCHELL

During the first week of May 1999, Kosovar refugees—
ethnic Albanians— came to the United States to seek refuge
from their war-torn country.

They are, by any reckoning, the wretched refuse: truly tired, poor, and yearning to breathe free. Emma Lazarus's words have been endlessly repeated to describe those who have fled to America's shores, but no group has better fit that portrait than the 453 men, women, and children who arrived last week at New Jersey's Fort Dix. Bone weary, emotionally spent, the refugees from Kosovo's killing fields filed silently, virtually expressionless, from a Boeing 747. There was no baggage in the jumbo jet's hold. The 249 adults, 195 children, and nine infants landed with nothing but the clothes on their backs, the stench of Macedonia's Stankovic camp in their noses, and memories that others can only imagine. They are penniless, but each owes Uncle Sam $350 for the cost of the flight—a debt that will be canceled if they return, eventually, to Kosovo. "We want to welcome them to America as we would have hoped that so many of our parents and grandparents were welcomed at Ellis Island," said Brig. Gen. Mitchell Zais, who heads the resettlement program.

The refugees are the vanguard of 20,000 ethnic Albanians who are slated to be brought to the United States in the next few weeks. Relief agencies will work to find them jobs and homes, and they will be eligible for permanent residency and, later, citizenship. So far, 12 nations

Children from Kosovo are bused to a refugee facility.

from Norway to Israel have taken in refugees from the conflict in Kosovo. But the West is only beginning to deal with Europe's greatest forced migration—and some of its worst atrocities—since World War II.

Those horrors are delineated in a report scheduled to be released this week by the U.S. State Department. It makes clear in spare and pitiless detail just how brutal and widespread Slobodan Milosevic's campaign of "ethnic cleansing" has been . . . more than 90 percent of Kosovo's ethnic Albanians have been forcibly expelled from their homes, and thousands of houses in more than 500 cities, towns, and villages have been damaged or destroyed.

Some 700,000 émigrés have fled to neighboring Albania, Macedonia, and Montenegro, creating massive shelter, food, and health problems in a region that has long been one of Europe's poorest. Life in the sprawling, fetid refugee camps has been widely documented. But an estimated 600,000 displaced Kosovars remain in even worse conditions inside their ravaged homeland, under Serbian guns and beyond the reach of relief workers and the media.

Many are hiding in isolated forests or valleys, where they suffer from severe food shortages. They survive in ramshackle encampments consisting of tents, crude shelters, tractors, flatbed trailers, and cars, hiding from Serbian soldiers as best they can. In some cases, Yugoslav Army units reportedly have flushed them out with helicopters—and tossed down grenades as they fled.

The State Department's draft report says there may already have been more than 4,000 victims of mass executions in at least 70 towns and villages. In a hellish roll call, the report alphabetically lists 60 places—from Bela Crkva to Zjum—where atrocities allegedly have occurred. It is a catalog of people used as human shields against NATO bombs and Kosovo Liberation Army attacks; families burned alive in their homes; organized rapes; and torture. Hundreds, and perhaps thousands, of men and boys have been marched away and since unseen, their fates unknown.

Far from Kosovo, meanwhile, a fortunate few survivors are gradually piecing their lives back together on a verdant Army post in New Jersey. A tiny harbinger of that return to normalcy came just one day after the first planeload of refugees arrived. Lebibe Karaliju, 21, gave birth to a 7-pound, 8-ounce boy. She told doctors she would name her son America.

May 17, 1999 ∾

Your Tired, Your Poor,

Your Undocumented Foreigners

Charles Osgood

It's clear that, given the chance, at least half of South and Central America would like to move to North America. Not to mention half of Asia, Africa, and assorted other continents. The reasons given are usually political, although one suspects that economic, rather than political, circumstances may be at the heart of it. It is simply not possible to open up all our borders and tell everybody in the world who wants to come here that they can. No place else in the world can afford to do it either, and no place does.

The degree to which America lifts her lamp of welcome depends on which immigration category you fall into. Basically, you have six kinds of people who want to move to the United States. You have:

1. Your tired.

2. Your poor.

3. Your huddled masses yearning to breathe free.

4. The wretched refuse of your teeming shore.

5. Your homeless.

6. Your tempest-tossed.

The U.S. immigration policy is different for each of these categories. Being tired of living in your own country is no longer considered a valid reason for being admitted for permanent residence in the United States. Even being sick and tired of it won't do. Being poor, which is the real reason a lot of people would like to move here, isn't considered a good enough reason, either. In fact, if you are rich you probably stand a better chance of being let in, since you can afford immigration lawyers, you can support yourself, and you're less likely to wind up on the public dole.[1]

As far as your huddled masses yearning to breathe free are concerned, unless they can prove they are being especially persecuted for some reason, the U.S. authorities will not automatically grant them political asylum. In fact, no matter how much they yearn to breathe free, the more huddled the masses are, the less likely the U.S. is to open the gate.

The United States is not in a position to accept the consequences of other countries' overpopulation problems. If you identify yourself as the wretched refuse of some teeming shore, you do not have a Chinaman's chance[2] of getting in. Actually a Chinaman's chances may be somewhat better than most, right now. If you were a Chinese student lucky enough to have been here when the crackdown came,[3] you are permitted, at least for now, to stay.

In spite of the nice words on the Statue of Liberty, in recent years the United States has not been able to cope with our own homeless situation, let alone absorb the homeless from elsewhere in the world. And being tempest-tossed does not make it any more likely you will be issued a green card.

The other day I mentioned aloud that you don't hear much any more about the Iron Curtain,[4] or about the Golden Door.[5] A young professional, the graduate of a distinguished American university, told me that she knew about the Iron Curtain but had never heard of the Golden Door. I can't say I was too surprised. ∽

1 **public dole:** welfare

2 **Chinaman's chance:** negative expression meaning little or no chance

3 **when the crackdown came:** In 1989, the Chinese government massacred hundreds of democratic demonstrators in Tiananmen Square and imposed martial law.

4 **Iron Curtain:** term referring to a barrier of Communism around Eastern European countries and the Soviet Union before Communism fell in the early 1990s

5 **Golden Door:** image of an "open" America for immigrants in search of a better life

"What Happened To The One We Used To Have?"

IMMIGRANTS

PAT MORA

wrap their babies in the American flag,
feed them mashed hot dogs and apple pie,
name them Bill and Daisy,
buy them blonde dolls that blink blue
eyes or a football and tiny cleats
before the baby can even walk,
speak to them in thick English,
        hallo, babee, hallo.
whisper in Spanish or Polish
when the babies sleep, whisper
in a dark parent bed, that dark
parent fear, "Will they like
our boy, our girl, our fine american
boy, our fine american girl?"

WINDOW III
1958
George Tooker

"MY FELLOW CITIZENS . . ."

PAUL GREENBERG

Don't confuse me with a TV preacher, but I want to share a blessing with you that I received May 1, 1985, about 11 o'clock in the morning. That's when, happy to accept an invitation from Judge George Howard, Jr., I got to deliver the address to newly naturalized citizens in his court-room at Little Rock.

Naturalization is a very special occasion—a kind of baptism, wedding, confirmation, commencement, Fourth of July, and Thanksgiving all rolled into one. As an official from the immigration service called out the names of the scores of people who were being naturalized that day, each new citizen would stand and respond with his or her country of origin. Ireland, Vietnam, Thailand, Germany, Chile, Iraq, Iran, Korea, Russia, Jordan, the Philippines, Mexico, India . . . you could almost hear the melt-ing pot still bubbling, and sense America being created anew. Their faces shone. I imagine mine did, too.

These new Americans have a lot to teach those of us whose citizen-ship is not as bright and fresh as theirs, or as arduously attained. Unlike them, many of us did not choose to be Americans. That distinction was a gift we received through no merit of our own, an act of unearned grace. And as Tom Paine[1] said at a time when there was some doubt about whether there would be an American nation, what we attain too easily, we esteem too lightly.

These new citizens are proof that America is still America, still draw-ing the hopeful from the ends of the earth in search of the American

---

1 **Tom Paine:** Thomas Paine, an American patriot and crusader for independence from England (1737–1809)

Naturalization ceremony, July 4, 1997, New York City.

dream. It was a joy to welcome them as others had welcomed my father and mother when this century was still young. I cherish an old photograph of the passengers aboard the S.S. *Argentina* when it arrived at the port of Boston with a shipload of immigrants February 10, 1921. If you look carefully through the faces, you can find a nineteen-year-old girl— broad Slavic features, pug nose, fair skin, dark hair drawn severely back, unsmiling in the photographic style of the day. A face indistinguishable from those of millions of other Eastern Europeans who flocked to the Golden Land between 1880 and 1920.

That is the face of my mother, Sarah the daughter of Paesach the miller, from outside the village of Mordt in eastern Poland. She was a country girl traveling alone to the New World with not much more than the clothes on her back. But if you look closely at the picture you can see, above the high cheekbones, in the eyes, the treasure she brought with her to this country. Those eyes are full of hope, and determination. If hope failed, determination would remain. And if determination failed, God would not. If she didn't fulfill the American dream, her children would, or her grandchildren, or their children.

My mother's Yiddish was piquant;[2] her English was, well, deliberate; and her silence was most eloquent of all. Whenever she would hear

2 **piquant:** sweetly charming

people blithely criticize America, she would give them what my brother, sister, and I called The Look. The message would be unmistakable: What do you know of America who only America know? The same look would freeze on her features when some armchair strategist[3] would speak blithely of war or hunger or poverty in her presence. Having grown up in the midst of the chaos that was the First World War, she did not take such things lightly.

Sometimes, when I examine that old photograph, or when I visit the national cemetery and battlefield at Vicksburg and drive past the still monuments that mark the site of so much bloody confusion and sacrifice and utter determination, or when I read a public-opinion poll that says most Americans consider themselves patriotic but not nearly so many believe they have a duty to do anything for their country, I wonder. I wonder if the determination, the readiness to sacrifice, the faith I see in that old photograph of my mother and her shipmates is still alive, and if my generation could do what she did. Could we put so much behind us, and reach out so far? Could we hope and struggle so long and so patiently with such moral certainty? I wonder.

And then, in a courtroom in Little Rock, Arkansas, I look at those rows of faces in all their different hues, and hear the Oath of Allegiance taken in a score or more of different accents, and it's clear that the Spirit of Liberty still lives, that America is still America. It is like seeing a varied and splendorous tapestry being endlessly woven.

I don't believe I told these new citizens anything they didn't already know. In fact, I probably didn't need to say anything; I think I could have just gone up to the rostrum[4] and looked at them for the next quarter of an hour, and they would have understood what I wanted to say. We have a special bond, we Americans.

May 5, 1985 ∾

---

3 **armchair strategist:** one who has a theory about how things
should be handled, but no practical experience

4 **rostrum:** raised platform for speakers

RESPONDING TO CLUSTER FIVE
Thinking Skill SYNTHESIZING

1. Each of the other clusters in this book is introduced by a question that is meant to help readers focus their thinking about the selections. What do you think the question for Cluster Five should be?

2. How do you think the selections in this cluster should be taught? Demonstrate your ideas by joining with your classmates to create discussion questions, lead discussions about the selections, develop vocabulary activities, and prepare a quiz.

REFLECTING ON *FROM THERE TO HERE:*
Essential Question SHOULD WE KEEP AMERICA'S IMMIGRATION DOOR OPEN?

Reflecting on this book as a whole provides an opportunity for independent learning and the application of the critical thinking skill, synthesis. *Synthesizing* means examining all the things you have learned from this book and combining them to form a richer and more meaningful view of the immigrant experience.

There are many ways to demonstrate what you know about immigration. Here are some possibilities. Your teacher may provide others.

1. After reading this book you should have a better idea of the issues related to immigration in the United States. For example, there are some who feel that the United States should strictly limit the number of immigrants that enter each year. Others believe that the doors should be open. Stage a debate in your class on the following issue.

   Resolved: The United States should close its doors to all but the most qualified applicants who can show that they will benefit the American economy and society.

2. Reread the essay at the beginning of this book, "Melting Pot or Salad Bowl?" Write a speech or an essay on whether or not America should be a melting pot or a salad bowl. Use some of the concept vocabulary from page 12 in your speech or essay. To help develop your final product, answer one or more of the following questions: Should American immigrants be required to give up their language, diet, dress, religion, or customs? What degree of cultural assimilation should immigrants undergo? What, if any, parts of immigrants' former cultural identity should they maintain?

3. Individually or in small groups, develop an independent project that demonstrates what you have learned about immigration. For example, you might give a presentation on the problems associated with assimilation or illegal entry. Other options might include a music video, dance, poem, performance, drama, or artistic rendering.

AUTHOR BIOGRAPHIES

JANET BODE Born in New York and sometimes called "the Studs Terkel of American teens," Janet Bode at first earned a living as a teacher in Germany, Mexico, and Florida. She also worked for the Girl Scouts of America. After a brutal gang rape, she turned to writing as a form of therapy. Once she began writing, she did not shy away from any topic, from sibling relationships to rape and death. Many of her books resulted from talking with teens about their problems. Bode's fourteen books for teenagers have received twenty-six major awards from the National Council for Social Studies, the American Library Association, the New York Public Library, and others. Bode died of breast cancer on December 31, 1999, at the age of 56.

MARTIN ESPADA The son of a political activist, Martin Espada was born and reared in New York's impoverished East Side neighborhood. He grew up participating in demonstrations for social justice. After becoming a lawyer, he worked as a tenants' rights advocate, but he also wrote and published poems in the tradition of Pablo Neruda and the poets of the Nuyorican scene. Espada's work has won the Paterson Poetry Prize and the PEN/Revson Fellowship, the Gustavo Myers Outstanding Book Award, and the Independent Publisher Book Award. Currently, he teaches writing at the University of Massachusetts, Amherst, where he writes essays, edits anthologies, and continues to write poems.

PAUL FLEISCHMAN As a child growing up in California, Paul Fleischman liked riding his bike and looking for found objects more than anything else in the world. When he grew up he worked as a carpenter, bagel baker, bookstore clerk, library aide, and proofreader before becoming a writer. His work, which spans many genres, has won Newbery awards, a Golden Kite award, and the Scott O'Dell award. Fleischman does not write for recognition but because he is, he says, "a maker at heart." He constructs his stories slowly and carefully, taking pleasure in every page. Recently Fleischman has begun writing for adults as well as children, but he has no intention of limiting his work to one group of readers.

RUSSELL FREEDMAN is a nonfiction writer who prefers to call himself a "factual writer," because writing about factual topics sounds more interesting than *not* writing about fiction. Freedman has written close to forty books on various topics, including animal behavior and the behavior of admirable human beings, such as Eleanor Roosevelt, Crazy Horse, and Abraham Lincoln. He has won dozens of awards for making science and history come alive. His books often include his carefully chosen photographs about his topics.

NICHOLAS GAGE Civil war broke out in his native Greece in 1948 when Nicholas Gage was a child. Communist insurgents were kidnapping children and sending them to re-education camps inside Communist territory. Nicholas and his three sisters eluded them when their mother arranged for them to escape to the United States. At age nine,

Nicholas went to live with his father in Massachusetts. His mother, who remained in Greece, was imprisoned, tortured, and executed. When Gage grew up, he became an investigative reporter for the *New York Times*. He returned to Greece and learned about his mother's fate, which led to the writing of his best-selling book, *Eleni*. Currently, Gage works full-time as a biographical and historical writer.

WILLIAM E. GEIST Born in 1945 in Champaign, Illinois, Bill Geist attended the University of Illinois at Champaign/Urbana. There he met his wife, Jody. They were married in 1970. In 1971, he graduated from the University of Missouri with a master's degree in communications. From 1972 to 1980 Geist was a reporter and columnist for the *Chicago Tribune*. In 1980 Geist joined the *New York Times*, where his "About New York" column appeared twice a week. Geist has been a correspondent for the CBS news program *Sunday Morning* since 1987, where his work was honored with an Emmy Award in 1992 for his report on the sixty-sixth anniversary of America's famed Route 66. Geist also contributes to *60 Minutes II* and is the best-selling author of six books, including *The Big Five-Oh: Facing, Fearing and Fighting 50* and the *New York Times* bestseller *Little League Confidential*, an account of his experience as a coach of his son and daughter's Little League teams. His biggest accomplishment, he says, comes from taking third in the Illinois State Fair Bake-Off.

MICHAEL GOLD Named Itzok Isaac Granich at birth, Michael Gold was born in 1894 in New York of Jewish immigrant parents. Deeply opposed to U.S. involvement in World War I, Gold moved to Mexico in 1917 to avoid the draft. Gold returned to New York in 1920 and pursued a life in publishing, writing, and editing numerous books about social issues before his death in 1967.

PAUL GREENBERG is a nationally syndicated conservative columnist for the Arkansas *Democratic Gazette* in Little Rock, Arkansas. His editorials have won the Pulitzer Prize, the Walker Stone Award, and the H. L. Mencken Award.

EMMA LAZARUS Born in 1849 to a prosperous Jewish-Portuguese family in New York City, Emma Lazarus began writing as a teenager. In 1886, her father published her first book of poems, entitled *Poems and Translations*. Lazarus was a contemporary of Ralph Waldo Emerson, who admired her writing and helped make Lazarus part of an elite circle of American writers. Lazarus was an advocate for Jewish immigrants escaping persecution in Europe and Russia, and many of her poems reflect that concern. Lazarus died of Hodgkin's disease at age 38. Her poem "The New Colossus, " which in 1904 was etched on the base of the Statue of Liberty, became one of the most often quoted poems in the English Language.

MILTON MELTZER Born in Massachusetts in 1915 to the children of Jewish immigrants, Milton Meltzer learned to read early in life. He does not recall how he learned to read, but does remember days spent at the library reading such stories as *The Arabian Nights* and *Gulliver's Travels*. A full scholarship paid Meltzer's way through Columbia University. After serving in the Army Air Force during World War II, Meltzer returned to the United States to work as a publicist and then a freelance writer and editor. In 1946, he published his first book, a pictorial history of Black Americans. Today, he has written more than seventy books, mostly nonfiction books for young adults. Many of his books have either won awards or been nominated for them, and several have been named Best Children's Book of the Year.

PAT MORA An author and poet of Mexican-American descent, Pat Mora has written more than 25 books of poetry, fiction, and nonfiction for children and adults. Her grandparents immigrated to the United States during the Mexican Revolution. They spoke only Spanish. Their daughter Estela, who was Pat's mother, grew up translating English into Spanish for her parents. Estela raised her daughter to be bilingual. Thus, many of Mora's books contain both English and Spanish text.

CHARLES OSGOOD Charles Osgood was born in New York and graduated from Fordham University with a degree in economics. He has performed with the Mormon Tabernacle Choir and played the piano and banjo with the New York Pops and Boston Pops orchestras, but he made his career in broadcast journalism. Osgood has been an anchor and reporter for the *CBS Morning News*, the *CBS Evening News with Dan Rather,* and the *CBS Sunday Night News.* The author of six books, Osgood has earned numerous awards for his work in broadcast journalism and a nationwide reputation as the "poet-in-residence" of CBS.

HELEN WAITE PAPASHVILY was a writer and her husband, **GEORGE PAPASHVILY**, was a sculptor. The two collaborated on many books with great success. They often made literary use of their own lives, including their experiences as new immigrants. George used both naïve and modern techniques in his sculptures and showed his work in several museums. Helen Waite Papashvily not only wrote but also taught and encouraged other writers. She was a devoted promoter of libraries. George died in 1978 at the age of 80, and Helen died in 1996 at the age of 89.

MARGARET POYNTER Growing up in a home full of readers and writers, Margaret Poynter always loved literature. Though she worked as a waitress, when the last of her four children entered high school, she quit her job and became a writer. Poynter has published a novel for children, *Crazy Minnie*, as well as her many popular biographies and historical fiction, such as *Killer Asteroids* and *Marie Curie: Discoverer of Radium.*

MICHAEL PUPIN Born on Oct. 4, 1858, in what is now Yugoslavia, Michael Pupin had parents who were determined that he receive a good education. Thus, he was sent to study at Pancevo (in the Republic of Serbia) and then Prague (the capital of the Czech Republic). After his father died, Pupin immigrated to the United States and eventually enrolled at Columbia College in New York. After graduating from Columbia, he continued his studies in England at Cambridge University and in Berlin, Germany. He then returned to Columbia to work as a teacher, physicist, and inventor. Pupin is best known for his work in telephony, telegraphy, electrical tuning, and X-ray radiation. His autobiography won the Pulitzer Prize. He died in New York City in 1935.

ADRIENNE RICH During her childhood, Adrienne Rich began writing poetry. She won the Yale Younger Poets Prize for her first published book. Rich's poems and essays are an outgrowth of her continuing investigation of radical themes. They question the value of tradition, patriarchy, and materialism, and they take a feminist point of view. Her work has received many awards, including the Ruth Lilly Prize, the *Los Angeles Times* Book Award, the Lambda Literary Award, the Poets' Prize, and a MacArthur Fellowship.

AL SANTOLI A noted historian and author, Al Santoli has served as an investigator for the U.S. House of Representatives POW/MIA Task Force. An oral historian and Vietnam veteran, he received three Purple Hearts. Santoli is an award-nominated best-selling author of military history, including *Everything We Had: An Oral History of the Vietnam War*. He is a noted specialist on security issues in the Asia-Pacific region. He has won both a Pulitzer Prize and an American Book Award. His areas of expertise include Chinese foreign and security policy, transnational crime and terrorism in Asia, and U.S.-Taiwan policy.

MICHAEL SATCHELL A senior writer for *Conservation Frontlines*, the magazine of Conservation International, a worldwide organization concerned with protecting our environment, Michael Satchell is also a consultant to the Humane Society and a writer for *U.S. News and World Report*. He has contributed a wide range of articles, including "Hunting for Good Will," a fascinating assessment of William Shakespeare (also known as Gulielmus Shakspere). His article *A View to a Kill: How Safari Club International Works to Weaken ESA Protection* can be viewed at www.hsus.org.

PATRICIA SMITH Born and raised in New York City, Patricia Smith attended Brown University. She graduated with a degree in American Civilization. She lived in Cairo, Egypt, for a year, where she fell in love with the Middle East and with travel in general. In 1996, she earned a master's in journalism from the Columbia University Graduate School of Journalism. She has worked as a newspaper reporter for *The Philadelphia Inquirer* and *The Star-Ledger* in New Jersey. She is now an editor at *The New York Times Upfront*, a news magazine for teenagers published by Scholastic, Inc. in cooperation with *The New York Times*. You can visit their site online at www.upfrontmagazine.com.

STEPHEN SONDHEIM The only child of a distant father and emotionally abusive mother, Stephen Sondheim was born in New York City in 1930. He grew up there and on a farm in Pennsylvania. As a youngster Sondheim spent as much time as possible at the home of his friend Jimmy Hammerstein, whose father, Oscar Hammerstein, was a master lyricist and playwright. Hammerstein mentored Sondheim, who also became a master lyricist and famous American theatrical composer. Sondheim is one of the few musical playwrights ever to have won the Pulitzer Prize for Drama.

ROBERTO SURO has been writing about Hispanic issues for almost thirty years. He began his career as a journalist for *Time* magazine and *The New York Times*, covering the Justice Department, the State Department, and other Washington beats. He also has worked as a foreign correspondent in Latin America, Europe, and the Middle East as well as a domestic correspondent in Chicago and Houston. Through his work in journalism and his own research, he has become an authority on Hispanic immigration to the United States. Currently, he works as the Executive Director of the Pew Hispanic Center in Southern California.

RONALD TAKAKI The grandson of Japanese plantation laborers in Hawaii, Ronald Takaki grew up keenly aware of his ethnic identity. As an adult he made the study of ethnicity a career, becoming a professor of ethnic studies at the University of California at Berkeley and an ardent advocate of acknowledging multiculturalism. Takaki helped found UCLA's centers for African American, Asian American, Chicano, and Native American studies, and was instrumental in establishing the requirement that all Berkeley students take an American cultures course in order to graduate.

YOSHIKO UCHIDA The daughter of immigrants, Yoshiko Uchida was born in Berkeley, California, in 1921 and embraced American life. She was a student at the University of California in Berkeley on December 6, 1941, when Japanese forces attacked Pearl Harbor. When the American government decided to place Japanese Americans in internment camps through the duration of World War II, Uchida taught school in one of the camps. After the war ended, she earned a master's degree. She taught for a time and then worked as a secretary to allow more time for writing. Many of Uchida's stories tell about life for the children of immigrants, including life in the internment camps. Yet, as she has noted, they are "about values and feelings that are universal."

GUSTAVUS VASSA Born Olaudah Equiano in 1745 in what is now Nigeria, Gustavus Vassa was kidnapped as a child and sold into slavery in the New World. There he labored for a sea captain and, later, a merchant. Over time he managed to purchase his freedom, but he remained a seaman and traveled the world, even attempting to reach the North Pole. He traveled to London, where he became involved in the movement to abolish slavery, which led to his writing and publishing his autobiography, *The Interesting Narrative of the Life of Olaudah Equiano, or Gustavus Vassa the African* in 1789. The book became a bestseller, furthered the cause of abolition, and also made Vassa a very rich man. He died in 1797, long before slavery was abolished in the United States.

JOHN WINTHROP Born in 1587 in England, where he attended college and studied law, John Winthrop became an extremely devout Puritan. He believed England was about to be punished by God for the wickedness taking place around him, so he obtained a charter to found the Massachusetts Bay Colony in the New World. As governor of the colony, Winthrop pursued moderation, at least by Puritan standards. He rarely allowed executions for heresy, and he opposed a movement to veil women. He is known today for his "City on a Hill" speech, which expressed the Puritan goal of creating a holy community and the Puritan principle that the wealthy had a duty to care for the poor. Winthrop was married four times and had at least fifteen children before his death in 1649.

ADDITIONAL READING

The African American Family Album, Dorothy and Thomas Hoobler. This wonderful collection of materials on the African American experience contains more than 150 rare photographs, first-hand accounts, profiles of famous African Americans, and more. Introduction by Phylicia Rashad. ©1995

American Dragons: Twenty-Five Asian-American Voices, Laurence Yep, ed. This anthology represents a variety of Asian American teenagers' voices speaking through poetry, stories, and selections from plays. All reflect on the challenges they faced as Asian American children of immigrant parents. ©1995

Behind the Mountains, Edwidge Danticat. Writing in the notebook her teacher gave her, thirteen-year-old Celiane describes life with her mother and brother in Haiti as well as her experiences in Brooklyn after they immigrate to be reunited with her father. ©2002

Beyond the Western Sea, Book One: The Escape from Home, Avi. Maura O'Connell, fifteen, and her brother, Patrick, twelve, escape Ireland with only the belongings in their bundles and tickets for ocean passage. Sir Laurence Kirkle, eleven, flees a life of privilege to seek justice. Together they seek freedom. ©1997

Beyond the Western Sea, Book Two: Lord Kirkle's Money, Avi. Patrick and Maura O'Connell are fleeing from the ravages of Ireland's potato famine to America. When they land in Lowell, Massachusetts, their dreams of America are filled with more perils as they try to survive. ©1997

Border Crossings: Emigration & Exile, Roger Rosen and Patra McSharry, eds. This outstanding multicultural title in the award-winning Icarus World Issues series confronts the problems faced by people forced to leave their homelands. Contains nonfiction and fiction essays and photographs. ©1992

Children of the River, Linda Crew. Having fled Cambodia four years earlier to escape the Khmer Rouge Army, seventeen-year-old Sundara is torn between remaining faithful to the customs of her own people while enjoying life in her Oregon high school as a "regular" American. ©1991

Cuba 15, Nancy Osa. Violet Paz, a Chicago high school student, reluctantly prepares for her upcoming "quince," a Spanish nickname for the celebration of an Hispanic girl's fifteenth birthday. ©2003

Dear Emma, Johanna Hurwitz. In her letters to a Vermont friend, Dossi, a Russian-Jewish immigrant living in the Lower East Side of New York City in 1910, shares her thoughts about her new brother-in-law, the diphtheria epidemic, and the Triangle Shirtwaist Factory fire. ©2002

Dragonwings, Laurence Yep. This story portrays the rich traditions of the Chinese community as it made its way in a hostile new world. Newbery Honor winner. ©1977

Esperanza Rising, Pam Munoz Ryan. Esperanza and her mother are forced to leave their life of wealth and privilege in Mexico to go work in the labor camps of Southern California on the eve of the Great Depression. ©2000

Fitting In, Anilú Bernado. Five bittersweet short stories about young Cuban girls who have immigrated to the United States and are confronting painful challenges. ©1996

Flight to Freedom, Ana Veciana-Suarez. Writing in the diary which her father gave her, thirteen-year-old Yara describes life with her family in Havana, Cuba, in 1967, as well as her experiences in Miami, Florida, after immigrating there to be reunited with some relatives. ©2002

Giants in the Earth, Ole E. Rolvaag. A giant novel about the peasant immigrants who broke the American wilderness under the plow. ©1991

The Grape Thief, Kristine L. Franklin. In 1925, in a small Washington State community made up of families from different ethnic backgrounds, twelve-year-old Cuss tries to stay in school as he watches those around him struggle with various financial difficulties. ©2003

Habibi, Naomi Shihab Nye. When fourteen-year-old Liyana Abboud, her younger brother, and her parents move from St. Louis to a new home between Jerusalem and the Palestinian village where her father was born, they face many changes and must deal with the tensions between Jews and Palestinians. ©1999

A House of Tailors, Patricia Reilly Giff. When thirteen-year-old Dina emigrates from Germany to America in 1871, her only wish is to return home as soon as she can. As the months pass and she survives a multitude of hardships living with her uncle and his young wife and baby, she finds herself thinking of Brooklyn as her home. ©2004

How I Became an American, Karen Gündisch. In 1902, ten-year-old Johann and his family, Germans who had been living in Austria-Hungary, board a ship to immigrate to Youngstown, Ohio, where they make a new life as Americans. ©2001

How the Garcia Girls Lost Their Accents, Julia Alvarez. Fifteen interrelated stories, unfolding back in time from 1989 to 1956, explore the dilemmas of four Latinas uprooted from a privileged island life and thrown into the unyielding big city. ©1992

Immigrant Kids, Russell Freedman. Text and contemporary photographs chronicle the life of immigrant children at home, school, work, and play during the late 1880s and early 1900s. ©1995

Journey of the Sparrows, Fran Leaper Buss with Daisy Cubias. Three Salvadoran children enter the country nailed in a crate in the back of a truck and journey to Chicago, where they share a crowded apartment and live in fear of being discovered by immigration officials. ©1993

Letters from Rifka, Karen Hesse. In letters to her cousin in Russia, twelve-year-old Rifka tells of her journey in 1919 to America, from the dangerous escape over the border to the journey through Europe and across the sea to the new country. ©1993

Lupita Manana, Patricia Beatty. To help her poverty-stricken family, thirteen-year-old Lupita leaves her Mexican fishing village and enters California as an illegal alien and starts to work while constantly on the watch for immigration authorities. ©1992

My Antonia, Willa Cather. This is the saga of an immigrant girl and her family, who come to Nebraska from Czechoslovakia. ©1995

New Kids in Town: Oral Histories of Immigrant Teens (formerly titled *New Kids on the Block: Oral Histories of Immigrant Teens*), Janet Bode. Eleven teenage immigrants tell their compelling stories in their own words. This book will promote a greater understanding and appreciation for the rich ethnic and cultural diversity upon which our country is based. ©1991

An Ocean Apart, a World Away, Lensey Namioka. Set in China in 1921, ten years after the revolution, sixteen-year-old Yanyan struggles to define a role for herself in two very different countries on either side of the Pacific. She helps carve a new path for generations of women after her. ©2002

Rain of Gold, Victor Villasenor. This story explores three generations of Villasenor's kin, their spiritual and cultural roots back in Mexico, their immigration to California, and their overcoming poverty, prejudice, and economic exploitation. ©1992

Tangled Threads: A Hmong Girl's Story, Pegi Shea. After ten years in a refugee camp in Thailand, thirteen-year-old Mai Yang travels to Providence, Rhode Island, where her Americanized cousins introduce her to pizza, shopping, and beer, while her grandmother and new friends keep her connected to her Hmong heritage. ©2003

Walk Across the Sea, Susan Fletcher. In late nineteenth-century California, when Chinese immigrants are being driven out or even killed for fear they will take jobs from whites, Eliza defies the townspeople and her father to help a Chinese boy. ©2001

When I Was Puerto Rican, Esmeralda Santiago. In this bittersweet story of a young girl trapped between two cultures, the author gives extraordinary insight into what it is like to be Puerto Rican, both on the island and as an immigrant in New York City. ©1994

Year of Impossible Goodbyes, Sook Nyul Choi. A young Korean girl survives the oppressive Japanese and Russian occupation of North Korea during the 1940s. Sookan and her family know their only hope for freedom lies in a dangerous escape to South Korea. ©1993

Acknowledgements

CONTINUED FROM PAGE 2   "The Hardships of a Greenhorn" from *From Immigrant To Inventor* by Michael Pupin. Copyright © 1923 by Charles Scribner's Sons, renewed 1951 by Varvara Pupin Smith. Reprinted by permission of Scribner, a Division of Simon & Schuster, Inc.

"Huddled Masses" by Michael Satchell, from *U. S. News & World Report*, May 17, 1999. Copyright © 1999 by U. S. News & World Report. Reprinted with permission.

From *Immigrant Kids* by Russell Freedman, copyright © 1980 by Russell Freedman. Used by permission of Dutton Children's Books, a division of Penguin Putnam, Inc.

"Immigrants" by Pat Mora is reprinted with permission from the publisher of *Borders* (Houston: Arte Público Press—University of Houston, 1986).

"Looking North" from *Strangers Among Us* by Roberto Suro. Copyright © 1998 by Roberto Suro. Reprinted by permission of Alfred A. Knopf, Inc.

"The Melting Pot Bubbles in Rego Park" by William E. Geist, published 1/1/87. Copyright © 1987 by The New York Times Co. Reprinted with permission.

"My Fellow Citizens" by Paul Greenberg, published May 5, 1985. Copyright © 1985. Distributed by the Los Angeles Times Syndicate. Reprinted with permission.

"The Pogroms Were All Around Us," an excerpt from *Number Our Days* by Barbara Myerhoff. Copyright © 1978 by Barbara Myerhoff. Reprinted by permission of Dutton, a division of Penguin Putnam, Inc.

"Prospective Immigrants Please Note," copyright © 1993, 1967, 1963 by Adrienne Rich, from *Collected Early Poems: 1950 - 1970* by Adrienne Rich. Reprinted by permission of W. W. Norton & Company, Inc.

#2 and #4 from *Songs of Gold Mountain: Cantonese Rhymes from San Francisco Chinatown* by Marlon K. Hom. Copyright © 1987 The Regents of the University of California. Reprinted by permission of the University of California Press.

"Tears of Autumn" by Yoshiko Uchida. From *The Forbidden Stitch*, edited by Shirley Geok-Lin Lim, Mayumi Tsutakawa, Margarita Donnelly. Copyright © 1989. Reprinted by permission of the publisher, Calyx Books.

"Tires Stacked in the Hallways of Civilization," from *City of Coughing and Dead Radiators* by Martin Espada. Copyright © 1993 by Martin Espada. Reprinted by permission of W. W. Norton & Company, Inc.

"The Tortilla Curtain," from *New Americans: An Oral History* by Al Santoli, copyright © 1988 by Al Santoli. Reprinted by permission of Viking Penguin, a division of Penguin Putnam, Inc.

Excerpt from "Von (age 20, Vietnamese)" from *New Kids on the Block: Oral Histories of Immigrant Teens* by Janet Bode. Copyright © 1989 by Janet Bode. Franklin Watts (hardback); Scholastic, Inc. (softback). Reprinted by permission of the author.

"You Are Only a Boy" from *The Uncertain Journey* by Margaret Poynter. Copyright © 1992 by Margaret Poynter. Reprinted by permission of Atheneum Books for Young Readers, an imprint of Simon & Schuster Children's Publishing Division.

"Your Tired, Your Poor, Your Undocumented Foreigners," from *The Osgood Files* by Charles Osgood. Copyright © 1986, 1987, 1988, 1989, 1990, 1991 by Charles Osgood. Reprinted by permission of Putnam Berkley, a division of Penguin Putnam, Inc.

Every reasonable effort has been made to properly acknowledge ownership of all material used. Any omissions or mistakes are not intentional and, if brought to the publisher's attention, will be corrected in future editions.